Discover the
Central Adirondacks

Four-Season Adventures in the
Heart of the North Woods

Discover the Central Adirondacks

Four-Season Adventures in the
Heart of the North Woods

Barbara McMartin

Second Edition

Prepared with the assistance of Dennis Conroy,
James C. Dawson, and Edythe Robbins

Backcountry Publications
Woodstock, Vermont

Marsh in Hoffman Notch

An Invitation to the Reader
Over time trails can be rerouted and signs and landmarks altered. If you find that changes have occurred on the routes described in this book, please let us know so that corrections may be made in future editions. The author and publisher also welcome other comments and suggestions. Address all correspondence to:

Editor
Discover the Adirondacks Series
Backcountry Publications
P.O. Box 175
Woodstock, VT 05091

Library of Congress Cataloging-in-Publication Data
McMartin, Barbara.
  Discover the Central Adirondacks: four-season adventures in the heart of the north woods/Barbara McMartin; prepared with the assistance of Dennis Conroy, James C. Dawson, and Edythe Robbins.—2nd ed.
    p. cm.
  Includes bibliographical references and index.
  ISBN 0-942440-50-1
  1. Hiking—New York (State)—Adirondack Mountains—Guide-books.
  2. Outdoor recreation—New York (State)—Adirondack Mountains—Guide-books. 3. Adirondack Mountains (N.Y.)—Description and travel—Guide-books. I. Title.
  GV199.42.N652A3443 1992
  796.5'09747'5—dc20   91-39517
                                                              CIP

© 1986, 1992 by Barbara McMartin
All rights reserved
Published by Backcountry Publications
A division of The Countryman Press, Inc.
Woodstock, Vermont 05091
Printed in the United States of America

Design by Leslie Fry
Typesetting and paste-up by Sunrise Composition
Layout by Barbara McMartin
Maps by Richard Widhu
All photographs by Barbara McMartin except p. 33, Pat Collier; p. 20, Edythe Robbins; pp. 91, 117, Dennis Conroy.

Cover: Moxham Mountain

Acknowledgments

As the *Discover the Adirondacks* series of regional guides has grown, so has the number of knowledgeable woods people who have worked with me, increasing also the role they play in producing and contributing parts of the books. As the lines that separate the guides evolved, I added several destinations so the *Discover* series would cover every part of the Adirondacks.

To research the Central area again for this revision, I walked all the areas that Dennis Conroy and Erwin Miller had explored for the first edition of 1986. This guide is larger than the earlier edition. The most exciting additions are several new bushwhacks, which I researched in the company of W. Alec Reid, Phil Terrie, Edythe Robbins, and Chuck Bennett.

Erwin Miller introduced me to the Hudson River Gorge Primitive Area, and he has contributed material on the river drivers. Dennis Conroy skied and wrote about parts of the area near Indian Lake and all of the Preston Ponds area. James C. Dawson, who is a geologist, wrote about the geology of the Hudson River Gorge. He was most helpful in exploring the Burroughs' caves. Edythe Robbins walked much of the area near Schroon Lake, discovering what turned out to be one of the region's best bushwhacks, and with her I explored several of the new bushwhacks in this edition.

Alec Reid not only walked with me, he again turned out excellent prints of all of this guide's black and white photos.

Background information came from many sources. Bill Roden filled me in on the history of Cheney Pond. F. B. Rosevear contributed information about early surveys, especially from the works of Colvin; and he contributed the origins of some Adirondack names.

Several DEC rangers helped with earlier editions and Bruce Coon contributed several hints for this revision.

Interesting bits of local history have come from Helen Donohue and John Paradis.

Jerold Pepper made available several important documents from the Library of the Adirondack Museum and Blue Mountain Lake and suggested sources which I never knew existed.

Many of these friends read portions of the guide. All of them contributed to the accuracy, but, more important, they helped give it the richness of detail that makes it a special kind of guide. I thank them all. They have not only helped me; they have done a superb job.

Moxham Mountain

Contents

Introduction	11
Trails near Schroon Lake	19
1. Severance Hill (*map I*)	24
2. Peaked Hills and Hints about Hoffman Mountain (*map I*)	26
3. Big Pond (*map I*)	28
4. North Pond and Jones Hill (*map I*)	32
5. East Branch Trout Brook (*map I*)	34
Irishtown, Loch Muller	35
6. The Split Glacial Erratic (*map I*)	37
7. Loch Muller to Big Marsh at Hoffman Notch (*map I*)	38
8. Loch Muller to Big Pond (*map I*)	40
9. Bailey Pond (*map I*)	42
10. Bailey Pond Inlet and Marion Pond (*maps I, III*)	42
11. Bailey Pond Inlet to Washburn Ridge (*map I*)	43
12. The 1808 Hoffman Cemetery (*map I*)	45
13. Muller Pond (*map I*)	46
14. Oliver Pond (*map I*)	46
North Creek to Tahawus—The Roosevelt Memorial Highway	47
15. Moxham Mountain (*map II*)	48
16. Stony, Big and Little Sherman Ponds, and Falls Brook to Irishtown (*map III*)	52
17. Rankin Pond (*map III*)	54
18. Hewitt Pond (*map III*)	55
19. Hewitt, Barnes, Center, and Stony Ponds Circuit (*map III*)	59
20. Lindsey Marsh (*maps III, IV*)	60
21. Boreas Circuit (*maps III, IV*)	61
22. Moose Pond Road (*maps III, IV*)	64
23. Vanderwhacker Mountain (*maps III, IV*)	64
24. Vanderwhacker Brook Stillwater (*map IV*)	65
25. Old Roadway to the Blue Ridge Road (*map IV*)	66

North Woods Club Road   67

26. The Railroad from the North Woods Club Road
to the Moose Pond Road (*maps III, V*)   70
27. The Burroughs Caves and Hot Water Pond (*map V*)   72
28. Nates and Grassy Ponds (*map V*)   74
29. Pine and Forks Mountains (*map V*)   76
30. Kettle Mountain (*map V*)   81
31. Blue Ledge and Huntley Pond (*map V*)   82

Indian Lake to Blue Mountain Lake to Long Lake   83

32. Cedar River and Pasley Falls (*map VI*)   86
33. Unknown Pond (*map VI*)   86
34. Pasley Falls and Elm Island (*map VI*)   87
35. McGinn Mountain (*map VI*)   90
36. Rock Lake and Rock River (*map VI*)   92
37. Rock Lake (*maps VI, VII*)   93
38. Rock Lake to Lake Durant (*maps VI, VII*)   94
39. Rock River Loop (*maps VI, VII*)   94
40. Tirrell Pond from the South (*map VII*)   95
41. Tirrell Pond from the West (*map VII*)   98
42. Blue Mountain (*map VII*)   99
43. East Inlet Brook (*map IX*)   101

West of Blue Mountain and Long Lakes   103

44. Castle Rock (*map VII*)   106
45. Blue Mountain Lake to Upper Sargent Pond (*maps VII, VIII*)   107
46. Lower Sargent Pond from Marion River Carry (*map VIII*)   108
47. South Pond (*map IX*)   112
48. Upper Sargent Pond from the North (*map VIII*)   113
49. Lower Sargent Pond via Grass Pond (*map VIII*)   114
50. Sargent Ponds loop via Middle Pond (*map VIII*)   115
51. Tioga Point to Lower Sargent Pond (*map VIII*)   116
52. Forked Lake (*map VIII*)   119
53. Owls Head Mountain and Lake Eaton (*map IX*)   122
54. Owls Head Pond (*map IX*)   123

Long Lake to the Northway—The Blue Ridge Road   125

55. Long Lake to Tirrell Pond (*map IX*)   126
56. Goodnow Mountain (*map X*)   129
57. Huntington Forest Nature Trail (*map X*)   132
58. Adirondack Visitors Interpretive Center at Newcomb (*map X*)   132
59. Wolf Creek (*map X*)   133
60. High Peaks View Picnic Area (*map X*)   135
61. Vanderwhacker Pond (*map IV*)   135
62. Cheney Pond (*map IV*)   135
63. Lester Flow on Foot (*map IV*)   137
64. Lester Flow by Canoe (*map IV*)   139
65. Blue Ridge Road to Irishtown (*maps III, IV*)   141
66. Cheney Pond Overlook (*map IV*)   143
67. Boreas Explorations (*map IV*)   143
68. Brace Dam (*map IV*)   145
69. Balancing Rock (*map IV*)   145
70. Hoffman Notch (*maps I, IX*)   146
71. Boreas Mountain (*map XI*)   148
72. Waterfall on the Branch   152

North River to Indian Lake   153

73. Along the Hudson River—The Greyhound Bus Stop (*map II*)   154
74. Ross, Whortleberry, and Big Bad Luck Ponds (*map V*)   156

References and Other Resources   161

Index   163

Introduction

THE CENTRAL ADIRONDACKS described in this guide is a rectangle bounded by some of the park's most scenic highways: the Northway from Pottersville to North Hudson; NY 28 from North Creek to Indian Lake; NY 30 from Indian Lake to Blue Mountain Lake and Long Lake; NY 28 N from Long Lake to Newcomb; and the beautiful Blue Ridge Road from the Northway at North Hudson to Newcomb. Raquette Lake and the Raquette River make a logical western boundary so a portion of the Sargent Ponds Wild Forest west of NY 30 is included in the guide. The rectangle also encompasses the Hudson River Gorge Primitive Area, the Hoffman Notch Wilderness Area, and the Blue Mountain and Vanderwhacker Wild Forests. The guide includes a trail on private land and one small and isolated triangle of Wild Forest north of the Blue Ridge Road, whose characters make them more appropriate here than with a description of the High Peaks to which they are adjacent.

While large portions of the rectangle are Forest Preserve, relatively little of the roadsides of the bordering highways are state land or have access to it. NY 28 N from North Creek to Newcomb bisects the rectangle and leads to numerous smaller roads which do lead to state land, but even here the pattern of ownership deprives the public of some of the most wonderful parts of the region. OK Slip Falls and OK Slip Pond, the confluence of the Indian and the Hudson, fabled Mink Pond, the Essex Chain Lakes, and Salmon Pond are all privately owned. Some of these will undoubtedly remain in private hands, but current state efforts to acquire the most fragile and most beautiful among them are certain to be realized in the near future. These additions to the Forest Preserve are so desirable, particularly in the Hudson River Gorge Primitive Area, that this guide mentions possible accesses, should the purchases be made.

Rather than dwelling on what is not open to the public, come and discover the surprising number of opportunities there are for those who love the out-of-doors. While you will not find the open summits of the great High Peaks region just to the north, there are several good mountain trails and secret cliff tops with distant views. The long, gentle routes that follow old roadways are great cross-country ski routes. Numerous ponds beckon for fishing and camping. The rivers are marvelous. The wild water of the Hudson and the Boreas are fabled, but the smaller rivers like Vanderwhacker Brook and Rock River and the stillwaters of the Boreas have a special charm. Stands of noble hardwoods mix with hemlock, spruce, and cedar to shelter the region's ponds and slopes. You may have to work to discover many of the region's destinations; but with the exception of two or three very popular spots, you will also find the heart of the quiet north woods secreted in dense forests and relatively unchanged from the time of first discovery a century and a half ago.

How to Use the *Discover* Guides

The regional guides in the *Discover the Adirondacks* series will tell you enough about the areas so that you can enjoy each one in many different ways at any time of year. Each guide will acquaint you with that region's access roads and trailheads, its trails and unmarked paths, some bushwhack routes and canoe trips, and its best picnic spots, campsites, and ski-touring routes. At the same time, the guides will introduce you to valleys, mountains, cliffs, scenic views, lakes, streams, and a myriad of other natural features.

Some of the destinations are within walking distance of the major highways that ring the areas while others are miles deep into the wilderness. Each description will enable you to determine the best excursion for you to enjoy the natural features you will pass—whether you are on a summer-day hike or a winter ski-touring trek. The sections are grouped in chapters according to their access points. Each chapter contains a brief introduction to that area's history and the old settlements and industries that have all but disappeared into the wilderness. Throughout the guide you will find accounts of the geological forces that shaped features of the land, a mention of unusual wildflowers, and descriptions of forest stands.

It is our hope that you will find this guide not only an invitation to know and enjoy the woods but a companion for all your adventures there.

MAPS AND NOMENCLATURE

The *Adirondack Atlas*, a map published by the City Street Directory of Poughkeepsie, New York, is the best reference for town roads, and it has the added advantage of identifying state land. In spite of the fact that it has not been updated to show recent acquisitions, it is a valuable aid where public and private lands are intricately mixed. The new *Adirondack North*

Introduction 13

Country Regional Map shows all state land, including purchases made through 1986. Copies may be obtained free of charge as long as the supply lasts by contacting Adirondack North Country Association, P O Box 148, Saranac Avenue, Lake Placid, NY 12946, phone 518-523-9820.

Accompanying this guide is a map showing all the routes mentioned. It is based on the new (1990) 7.5 by 15-minute metric, United States Geological Survey maps, reduced 50 percent to give a scale of 1 mile to 1.25 inches. It is adequate for the marked trails. You may still want to carry the larger scale maps for the more difficult bushwhacks; but note that while the land contours and streams are much more accurately shown than in earlier maps, there are serious errors in the locations of some trails on the new USGS. These errors have been corrected in the accompanying map. The maps used are those for Forked Lake, Raquette Lake, Deerland, Blue Mountain Lake, Newcomb, Dutton Mountain, Blue Ridge, and Schroon Lake.

Maps are available locally in many sporting goods stores. You can order maps from USGS Map Distribution Branch, Box 25286, Denver Federal Center, Denver, CO 80225. They are currently more easily obtained from a private source, Timely Discount Topos. You can call them at 1-800-821-7609; they will ship your maps as soon as they receive your check.

This guide uses the spellings given in the USGS, but local variations are noted.

DISTANCE AND TIME

Distance along the routes is measured from the USGS survey maps and is accurate to within ten percent. It is given in miles, feet, or yards except where local signs use metric measure. Distance is a variable factor in comparing routes along paths or bushwhacks. Few hikers gauge distance accurately, even on well-defined trails.

Time is given as an additional gauge for the length of routes. This provides a better understanding of the difficulty of the terrain, the change of elevation, and the problems of finding a suitable course. Average time for walking trails is 2 miles an hour, 3 miles if the way is level and well-defined; for paths, 1½ to 2 miles an hour; and for bushwhacks, 1 mile an hour.

Vertical rise refers to the change in elevation along a route up a single hill or mountain; *elevation change* generally refers to the cumulative change in elevation where a route crosses several hills or mountains.

14   *Discover the Central Adirondacks*

   A line stating distance, time, and vertical rise or elevation change is given with the title of each section describing trails and most paths, but not for less distinct paths and bushwhacks for which such information is too variable to summarize. Distance and times are for *one way only* unless otherwise stated. The text tells you how to put together several routes into longer treks that will occupy a day or more.

TYPES OF ROUTES

Each section of this guide generally describes a route or a place. Included in the descriptions are such basic information as the suitability for different levels of woods experience, walking (or skiing, paddling, and climbing) times, distances, directions to the access, and, of course, directions along the route itself. The following definitions clarify the terms used in this book.

   A route is considered a *trail* if it is so designated by the New York State Department of Environmental Conservation (DEC). This means the trail is routinely cleared by DEC or volunteer groups and adequately marked with official DEC disks. *Blue disks* generally indicate major north-south routes, *red disks* indicate east-west routes, and *yellow disks* indicate side trails. This scheme is not, however, applied consistently throughout the Adirondacks.

   Some trails have been marked for *cross-country skiing*, and new *pale yellow disks with a skier* are used. *Large orange disks* indicate *snowmobile trails*, which are limited to some portions of Wild Forest Areas. Snowmobiles are permitted on them in winter when there is sufficient snow cover. The guide indicates those trails not heavily used where skiing and snowmobiling may be compatible, but a skier must always be cautious on a snowmobile trail. Hikers can enjoy both ski and snowmobile trails.

   A *path* is an informal and unmarked route with a clearly defined foot tread. These traditional routes, worn by fishermen and hunters to favorite spots, are great for hiking. A path, however, is not necessarily kept open, and fallen trees and new growth sometimes obliterate its course. The paths that cross wet meadows or open fields often become concealed by lush growth. You should always carry a *map and a compass* when you are following an unmarked path, and you should keep track of your location.

   There is a safe prescription for walking paths. In a group of three or more hikers, stringing out along a narrow path will permit the leader to scout until the path disappears, at which point at least one member of the party should still be standing on an obvious part of the path. If that hiker remains standing while those in front range out to find the path, the whole group can continue safely after a matter of moments.

Hikers in the north country often use the term *bushwhack* to describe an uncharted and unmarked trip. Sometimes bushwhacking literally means pushing brush aside, but it usually connotes a variety of cross-country walks.

Bushwhacks are an important part of this regional guide series because of the shortage of marked trails throughout much of the Adirondack Park and the abundance of little-known and highly desirable destinations for which no visible routes exist. Although experienced bushwhackers may reach these destinations with not much more help than the knowledge of their location, I think most hikers will appreciate these simple descriptions that point out the easiest and most interesting routes and the possible pitfalls. In general, descriptions for bushwhacks are less detailed than those for paths or trails; it is assumed that those who bushwhack have a greater knowledge of the woods than those who walk only marked routes.

Bushwhack is defined as any trip through the woods without a trail, path, or the visible foot tread of other hikers and without markings, signs, or blazes. It also means you will make your way by following a route chosen on a contour map aided by a compass and using streambeds, valleys, abandoned roads, and obvious ridges as guides. Most bushwhacks require not only navigating by contour map and compass but an understanding of the terrain.

Bushwhack distances are not given in precise tenths of a mile. They are estimates representing the shortest distance one could travel between points. This reinforces the fact that each hiker's cross-country route will be different, yielding different mileages.

A bushwhack is said to be easy if the route is along a stream, a lakeshore, a reasonably obvious abandoned roadway, or some similarly well-defined feature. A short route to the summit of a hill or a small mountain can often be easy. A bushwhack is termed moderate if a simple route can be defined on a contour map and followed with the aid of a compass. Previous experience is necessary. A bushwhack is rated difficult if it entails a complex route, necessitating advanced knowledge of navigation by compass and by reading contour maps and land features.

Compass directions are given in degrees from magnetic north and in degrees from true north. The text will usually specify which reference is used; but if no reference is given, the degrees refer to magnetic north.

The guide occasionally refers to old blazed lines or trails. The word *blaze* means to mark as by cutting. Early loggers and settlers made deep slashes in good-sized trees with an axe to mark property lines and trails. Hunters and fishermen have also often made slashes with knives and, though they are not so deep as axe cuts, they can still be seen. It is now, and has been for many years, illegal to deface trees in the Forest Preserve in this manner. Following an old blazed path for miles in dense woods is often a challenging but good way to reach a trailless destination.

You may see yellow paint daubs on a line of trees, also referred to in the text as paint blazes. These lines usually indicate the boundary between private and public lands. Individuals have also from time to time used different colors of paint to mark informal routes.

Although it is not legal to mark trails on state land, this guide does refer to such informally marked paths.

All *vehicular traffic*, except snowmobiles on their designated trails, is *prohibited* in the Forest Preserve. Vehicles are allowed on town roads and some roads that pass through state land to reach private inholdings. These roads are described in the guide, and soon the DEC will start marking those old roads that are open to vehicles. Most old roads referred to here are town or logging roads that were abandoned when the land around them became part of the Forest Preserve. Now they are routes for hikers, not for vehicles.

Cables have been placed across many streams by hunters and other sportsmen to help them cross in high water. The legality of this practice has been challenged. Some may be quite safe to use; others are certainly questionable. Using them is not a recommended practice so when this guide mentions crossing streams to reach some of the hikes, you are urged to do so only when a boat can be used or when you can wade across in low water.

Protecting the Land

Most of the land described in these guides is in the Forest Preserve, land set aside a century ago. No trees may be cut on this state land. All of it is open to the public. The Adirondack Park Agency has responsibility for the Wilderness, Primitive, and Wild Forest guidelines that govern use of the Forest Preserve. Care and custody of these state lands is left to the Department of Environmental Conservation, which is in the process of producing Unit Management Plans for the roughly 130 separate Forest Preserve areas.

Camping is permitted throughout the public lands except at elevations above 4000 feet and within 150 feet of water or 100 feet of trails. In certain fragile areas camping is restricted to specific locations, and the state is using a new No Camping disk to mark fragile spots. *Permits* for camping on state lands are needed only for stays that exceed three days or for groups of more than ten campers. Permits can be obtained from the local rangers, who are listed in the area phone books under New York State Department of Environmental Conservation.

Only dead and downed wood may be used for *campfires*. Build fires at designated fire rings or on rocks or gravel and only when absolutely necessary; preferably, carry a small stove for cooking. Fire is dangerous and can travel rapidly through the duff or organic soil, burning roots and spreading through the forest. Douse fires with water, and be sure they are completely out and cold before you leave.

Private lands are generally not open to the public though some individuals have granted public access across their land to state land. It is always wise to ask before crossing private lands. Be very respectful of private landowners so that public access will continue to be granted. Never enter private lands that have been posted unless you have the owner's permission. Unless the text expressly identifies an area as state-owned Forest Preserve or private land whose owner permits unrestricted public passage, the inclusion of a walk description in this guide does not imply public right-of-way.

Burn combustible trash and carry out everything else.

Most *wildflowers and ferns* mentioned in the text are protected by law. Do not pick them or try to transplant them.

Safety in the Woods

It is best *not to walk alone*. Make sure someone knows where you are heading and when you are expected back. Wherever there is a trailhead *register*, be sure you sign in and out and note your planned route and destination.

Carry water or other liquids with you. Not only are the mountains dry, but the recent spread of *Giardia* makes many streams suspect. I have an aluminum fuel bottle especially for carrying water; it is virtually indestructible and has a deep screw that prevents leaking.

Carry a small *day pack* with insect repellent, flashlight, first aid kit, emergency food rations, waterproof matches, jackknife, whistle, rain gear, and a wool sweater, even for summer hiking. Wear layers of wool and waterproof clothing in winter and carry an extra sweater and socks. If you plan to camp, consult a good outfitter or a camping organization for the essentials. Better yet, make your first few trips with an experienced leader or with a group.

Always carry a *map and compass*. You may also want to carry an altimeter to judge your progress on bushwhack climbs.

Wear *glasses* when bushwhacking. The risk to your eyes of a small protruding branch makes this a necessity.

Carry *binoculars* for birding as well as for viewing distant peaks.

Use great care near the *edges of cliffs* and when *crossing streams* by hopping rocks in the streambed. Never bushwhack unless you have gained a measure of woods experience. If you are a novice in the out-of-doors, join a hiking group or hire the services of one of the many outfitters in the north country. As you get to know the land, you can progress from the standard trails to the more difficult and more satisfyingly remote routes.

Bears have become a problem throughout the Adirondacks and they are especially bothersome to campers near some of the more popular camping areas. There are some things you can do to foil bears: keep all food in sealed containers and hang all food overnight in "bear bars," suspended on a rope thrown between two trees at least 15 feet apart, with the bear bag at least 10 feet from the ground. Do not keep food in your tent. A few bears have learned to attack ropes to get at the bags so even this may not be a fool-proof solution. In some areas it is recommended that you not sleep in clothing that you wear while cooking. It may be wise to suspend your pack as well as your food sack as even the pack carries food odors.

Bears are not a problem during the daytime and only at night if they detect food. If bears do come near your campsite, clanging pots and pans may scare them away.

Trails near Schroon Lake

SCHROON LAKE WAS said to be "one of the wildest and most beautiful Lakes in the State of New York, and probably in the United States. . . . It is peculiarly American in its character, being both wild and picturesque, and one which the artist delighted to portray." These words accompany an engraving by Thomas Cole of Scaroon or Schroon Lake in the 1868 work *A Landscape Book*. Cole and Asher Durand visited the lake in the summer of 1837. Cole painted the wild and romantic beauty of the forest and lake at a time when most of the Adirondacks was unknown territory.

On Governor Tryon's 1779 map, the lake is shown with the name "Scaron," giving credence to the theory that its name is derived from the French and was meant to honor the beauteous French widow of the poet Scarron, who later married Louis XIV.

B. F. DeCosta's 1869 travel book *Lake George* describes the mountains to the west and northwest of Schroon Lake as the Schroon Mountains. The area is now called the Hoffman Notch Wilderness, and the mountains are the Blue Ridge Range. The slopes are heavily wooded with twilight sheltering a world of moss and fern and fragrant forest. No trails reach the highest of these wooded peaks. There are no open summits and only one or two cliffs from which to enjoy any distant views. The interior remains the silent and mysterious wilderness as it was when Cole and Durand first saw it.

Before you begin to explore the region's trails, you might wish to stop at the Natural Stone Bridge and Caves west of Pottersville. This commercial tourist attraction is the place to begin to understand the area's geological origins. Trout Brook, which winds through early chapters of this guide, has cut caves and grottos in the Grenville rock. Marked paths guide you along the brook and signs describe the forces of nature that created the spectacular scenery. Only one thing is missing—the stone bridge has washed away. When you visit the site, reflect on these words from Thomas Cole's diary to recreate the scene as he saw it.

> We descended into a woody valley and soon heard dashing of water and were on the banks of Trout Brook which enshadowed by lofty and overhang-

ing trees in this place dashes over iron-stained rocks and forms a picturesque waterfall then making a sudden turn plunges into yawning caverns. The rock at the mouth of this cave was 50 or 60 feet high and forms a stupendous arch. Above are wild hanging woods, below the brawling stream seeking its subterranean course. . . . The first impression of the beholder is that the sides of the craggy mountains have been rent and fallen across the narrow defile in gigantic ruins—this may partly be the fact but we soon perceive that the waters themselves have perforated the mighty masses of stones which is of a crumbly nature. . . . We descended and entered [a cavern below]. Soon the eye became accustomed to the dim light and perceived a torrent falling from the roof of the cave breaking and foaming over jagged rocks and again disappearing beneath our feet. In this cave beautiful spars are found and crystals of various hues. We ascended again and proceeded a little farther in the light of the sun, but soon behold in a deep hollow amid moss grown rocks a deep stream of pitchy darkness and smooth current. The water whirls round as though loathe to plunge again into subterranean channels. . . . We now proceeded to what is called the Wolf's cave. It is a low cave without water extending 40 or 50 feet under a roof of rock spangled with crystals—garnets— the birchbark torches which we have gave a rich tone of colour to all around. We now descended to where an arch of stone came that opens under a Gothick arch of rock. The arch rises from a still pool whose asphaltick coloured waters spread through the hollow chambers still as death. At a short distance from this the stream again issues into the light of day beneath two arches that open at the bases of wall-like precipices. . . . It looks almost as though chisselled by the hand of man, being a complete Roman arch. . . . The stream comes from the cavernous recesses gently as though it had slept in the profound darkness of the earth. The tones of colour of the rocks and the water are extremely beautiful here, rich grays and browns—the gliding water throws the reflected sunbeams far into the cavern and the caverns cast their sombre shadows far over the waters. Tangled wood roots and giant trunks overhang precipices of the secluded glen in savage and fantastic forms.

A second way to become acquainted with the area is a drive along NY 9 north of Schroon Lake as far as the bridge over the Schroon. On the east side of the road, north of the bridge, there is a public picnic spot known as Schroon Falls. The falls are small; but the swimming hole below them is cool and inviting and the picnic spot is a nice place to stop.

After a visit to the falls and the Natural Stone Bridge and Caves along Trout Brook and the brief introduction to Cole's romantic view of the region, you will be ready to explore the mountains west of Schroon Lake. The first thing you will notice is that access to the region from the east was cut off by the Northway. Culverts under the Northway with access from NY 9 will start you on your way.

View of Hoffman Mountain across North Pond

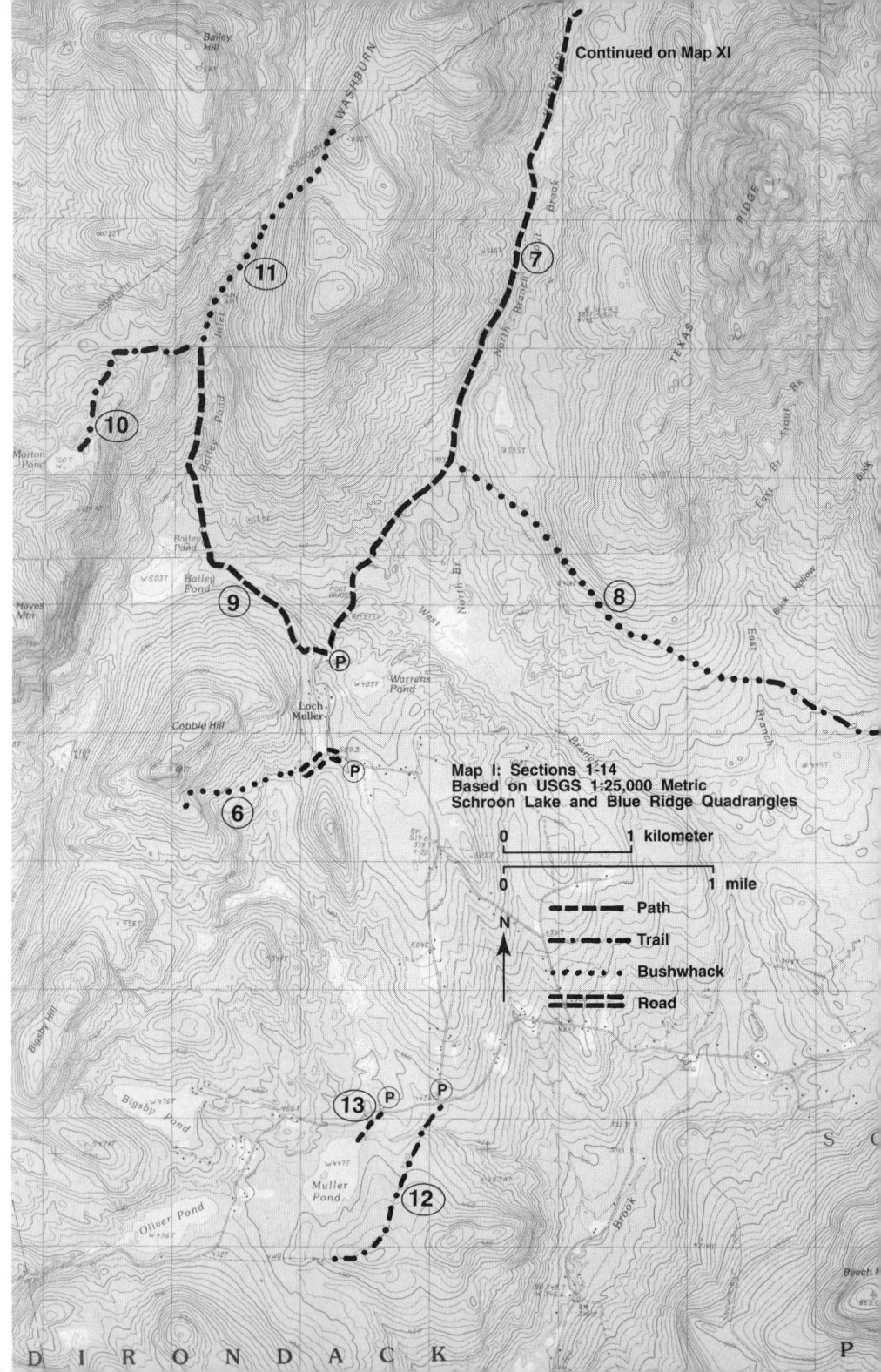

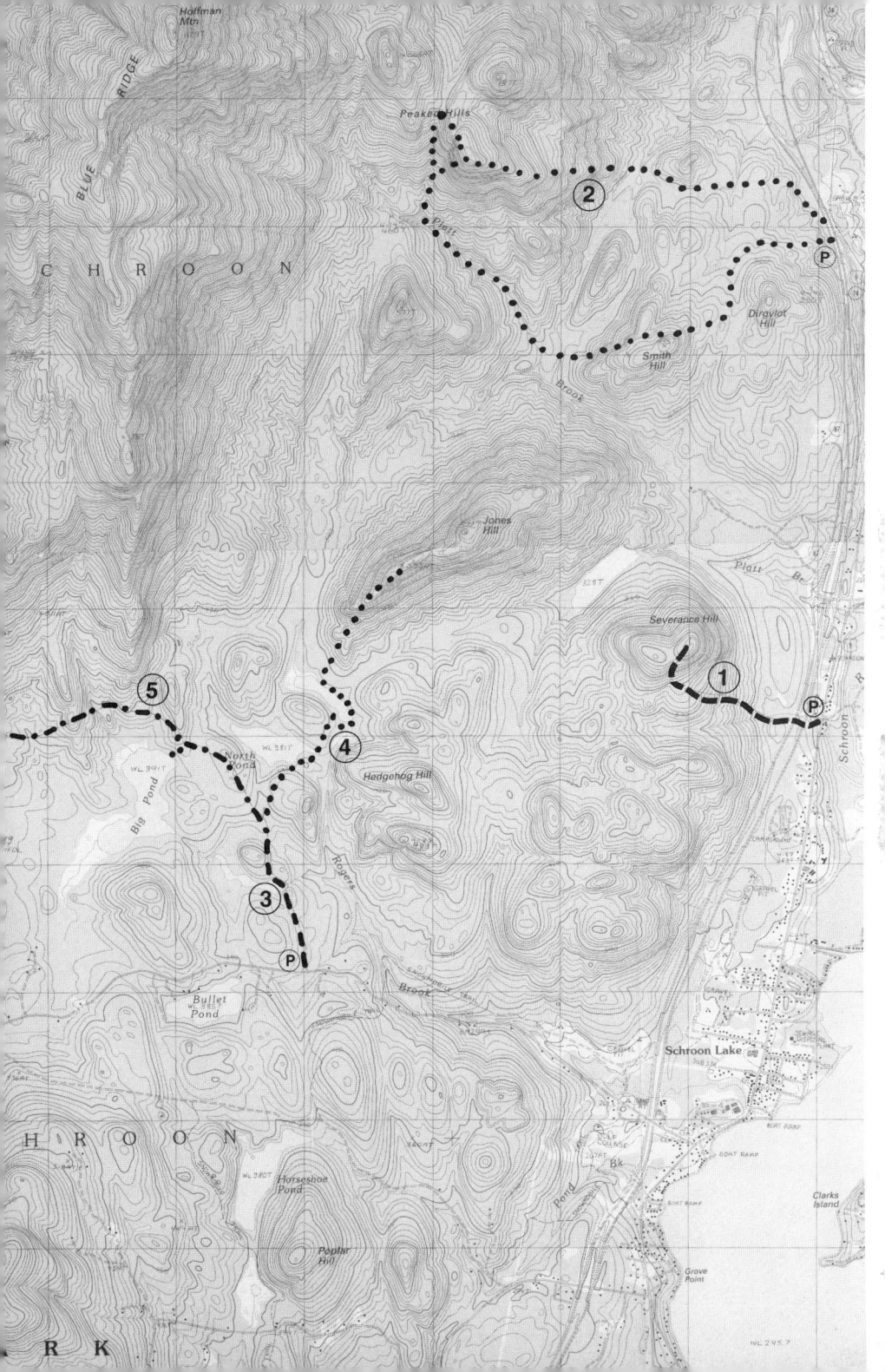

1 Severance Hill

Marked trail, hiking, snowshoeing
2 miles round trip, 2 hours, 735 feet (230 meters) vertical rise,
map I

Severance Hill is a small mountain (elevation 500 meters) on the west side of Schroon Lake and on the very eastern edge of the Blue Ridge. Its access and the panorama it commands are to the area east of the Hoffman Notch Wilderness. The trailhead is on NY 9 and 0.6 mile south of Northway entrance 28. West of the ample parking area is a narrow path leading through tunnels under the Northway.

The forest cover is a taste of what the Hoffman Notch Wilderness offers: cedars shading the lower slopes with tall hemlocks and pines and also cedars above. These give way on the higher slopes to oaks which are dominant in the lowland Adirondacks on dryer hillsides.

The trail is yellow marked and very easy to follow. It circles the south flanks of the mountain and heads north to the summit ridge. The first vantages overlook the Pharaoh Lake Wilderness; the most northerly looks toward Paradox Lake and the mountains of the Hammond Pond Wild Forest. Fire created the open patches on the summit, and for a time the grasses and low herbs here were mowed to preserve the view. In the past few years scrubby trees have begun to fill in, limiting the best views.

The only disappointment with the hill is the fact that it does not have an overlook toward the region covered by this guide. This is compensated by the fact that the hill is on the edge of the major migration area for small birds, and early spring birding for warblers is delightful.

A quarter mile from the summit you may spot an unmarked right fork to an old roadway. This was at one time marked by blue DEC trail markers and leads south toward Hoffman Road, where its beginning is now posted. A western fork from this path, about a mile from Hoffman Road, leads to open rocks on Hedgehog Hill. From here there is a nice view of the south end of Schroon Lake. The route toward Hedgehog Hill is on state land; but the southern half of that hill is private land so no through route is possible.

Open rock means easy walking on the summits of Peaked Hills

2 Peaked Hills and Hints about Hoffman Mountain

Bushwhacks, map I

Hoffman Mountain's name probably derives from the survey conducted in 1793 of lands in Schroon and Minerva townships for Anthony Hoffman. It was sometimes called Schroon Mountain. Artistically and visually it was one of the most impressive Adirondack mountains known to early visitors. Thomas Cole's 1838 painting of the mountain (he called it Schroon Mountain) is considered one of the artist's finest wilderness landscapes.

Cole wrote in his diary about a walk to view the mountain range to the west of Schroon Lake:

> We climbed a steep hill on which many sheep were at pasture and gained a magnificent view, below us lay a beautiful little lake embossomed in the hills and the perfect mirror of the surrounding woods. Beyond were hills of gradual ascent partially cleared of wood and beyond these the pyramid of Schroon [Hoffman] Mountain lifted its head aloft into the sky. We sketched here, but the cleared hills beyond the pond nearer the great mountain promised such an opportunity for a more complete view of the mountain that we could not resist the temptation, and the formation of the land seemed to indicate a lake beyond those hills at the foot of the mountain. This would be glorious we thought, and enthusiasm drew us on. We dashed down the hill toward the pond, skirted its shore through swampy forest, scrambled through the black logs of a recent burning, arrived at the new clearing, passed a log house or two . . . We climbed the topmost knoll of the clearing trampling down the luxuriant clover and beneath some giant denizens of the forest whose companions had all been laid low by the destroying axe—we eagerly looked towards west. . . . The hoary mountain rose in silent grandeur, its dark head clad in a dense forest of evergreen cleaving the sky a star-pointing pyramid—some distance from the summit that black uniform forest, the individual trees of which could scarcely be distinguished from distance and closeness, broke into lawn-like openings, green velvety descents. These gave place below to glistening side of rock and barren precipices. . . . Below stretched to the mountain's base a mighty mass of forest not broken . . . Here we felt the sublimity of untamed wilderness and the majesty of eternal mountains.

Hoffman Mountain's lofty peak created a feeling of vastness and awe, which the artist translated into a scene of mystery and danger, obscurity and solitude. Those attributes, which inspired the Hudson River painters, still cling to the mountain whose summit remains unscarred by trails.

Because of private land, there are, at present, no good accesses to the east side of the Blue Ridge Range and Hoffman Mountain, even by bushwhacking. However, the one access, which can lead you to the Peaked Hills, is also an approach used to reach Hoffman. Hoffman, with its dense cover, lack of views, and minimum eleven-hour bushwhack, attracts few climbers; and even those who have climbed it recently claim, "never again." You can obtain a good feeling for the Blue Ridge Range by climbing the Peaked Hills; and, if Hoffman still invites you, you can use the experience gained approaching Platt Brook as the start of that bushwhack.

Actually, the Peaked Hills, a cluster of three summits, one of which is faced with magnificent cliffs, are a delightful destination in themselves in spite of their low elevation, which ranges from 648 to 720 meters (2074 to 2304 feet), and the fact they are totally overshawdowed by Hoffman (1129 meters or 3613 feet). The beginning of the bushwhack is more difficult than it ought to be, mostly because it is not easy to get to public land along Platt Brook without using the most direct route over private land.

Park well off the edge of NY 9, 1.7 miles north of Northway exit 28. To the left of the entrance to the gravel pit is a dirt road that heads west to power lines, then north under the power lines for a five-minute walk to the tunnel under the Northway. The dirt road continues as a foot path, first climbing generally west to a T intersection with an old tote road that runs north-south or parallel with the Northway. Turn left (south) at the T and in about ten minutes you come to a small field with a path going right (west) from the tote road. If you continue straight (south) on the tote road—the longer route—the path follows an old road fairly steeply uphill to a field that was an old farm site. Continue southwest out of the field, climbing steeply, then descend around the side of Smith Hill. Through the trees you have views of Peaked Hills and Hoffman on the descent. There is a marvelous swamp at the bottom of the hill—great sphagnum and other mosses. Cross it at its narrowest, staying to the right and climbing to slightly higher ground. Contour around the low hillside, angling west, and you will reach Platt Brook, where there is a surprisingly good footpath.

Alternatively, turn right (west) and stay on the path until the path disappears. Then bushwhack west descending to the swamp described above. On the descent you will see Hoffman through the trees. After crossing the swamp, bushwhack due west and listen for the sound of running water. That will be Platt Brook. Head straight for it. If finding Platt Brook is difficult, the rest is very easy. Follow the path up Platt Brook (this route is also the best guide to starting up Hoffman). The path winds back and forth across the brook depending on the steepness of the banks. After twenty minutes, you reach an island in the brook. On the northwest side of the island there is an enigmatic sign on a maple tree reading "Apple Tree." A small brook joins Platt Brook in this vicinity; the first major confluence is a half mile farther upstream. Here, in a deep draw, is a brook draining the cleft in the Peaked Hills. Follow it north; it quickly splits into several smaller streams so always pick the easternmost stream. The sensible thing to do is to follow this course to the cleft; then climb out of it heading southeast toward the highest of the Peaked Hills.

When you get a bit more than halfway up the draw to the cleft from Platt Brook, you may be tempted to climb straight up the southeastern Peaked Hill. It is possible to scale the slopes because open rock begins almost immediately. But, watch out for the slippery patches of red pine needles that separate the open rock slabs.

A chain of open patches just below the top of the hill leads you back east. The views are mostly south, and, as you descend along the ridgeline, the views become more westerly. You see parts of Schroon Lake, Pharaoh Mountain, and most of the cliff-faced summits of the northern part of the Pharaoh Lake Wilderness. Immediately to the south is an unnamed pyramidal hill; to the east of it lies Jones Hill (section 4); and beyond them lies the mass of Green Mountain.

To descend, continue east, just below the ridgeline. The sheerest cliffs are beneath you after you have walked several hundred yards along the ridge. The descent is surprisingly easy, for the forest is very open and bare patches continue until you are almost in the valley that lies to the east. When you do reach that valley, you should cross a very small stream that flows north. Pick a compass course generally east, circling around a knob, across a second stream, then contouring southeast around the slopes of the hill that borders the Northway. This generally easterly course takes you to the Northway north of the tunnel. Stay on the grass slopes away from the highway to walk to the tunnel.

The climb as described is over 3 miles long and takes an equal number of hours; the return is less than 2.5 miles and takes about two hours if you have no trouble finding the routes.

3 Big Pond
Path, camping, hiking, cross-country skiing
1.6 miles, 50 minutes, relatively level, map I

Hoffman Road heads west from the village of Schroon Lake and climbs 500 feet in 4 miles. The eastern portion is bordered by private lands, but you reach state lands at 2.1 miles. Here a DEC sign on the north side of

Hoffman Road marks the end of an old road that leads to Big Pond. This route was once part of a snowmobile trail from Loch Muller (see section 8); and although it is not now marked and maintained, the portion to Big Pond is easy to follow. There is not much room to park beside Hoffman Road, but there are safe pullouts nearby.

Take the left fork in the reforestation area after a five-minute walk from the road. Within fifteen minutes you reach a bridge over the outlet of an extensive marsh. A large beaver dam on the stream flowing through the marsh—the outlet of Big Pond—currently floods the marsh, creating a new, fair-sized pond. A short distance east of here, the outlet joins Rogers Brook. Big Pond was originally named Rogers Pond.

There is good walking along the roadway, which continues its course of just west of north beyond the dam. The trail is through a red pine plantation with a few clumps of cedar beside the trail. Look for an immense clump of cedar and a pile of rock which may be a tailings pit— your clue to North Pond and Jones Hill (section 4). This point is less than ten minutes beyond the beaver flow and under a mile from Hoffman Road. Its beginning is quite concealed—with a log across it. The fork is in a small open area with some big birch nearby but few other obvious signs.

You continue northwest toward Big Pond. The roadway becomes indistinct, and the route is now a narrow path continuing through a wet area. Watch for the point where the path angles west in a hemlock stand. Three hundred yards beyond, where the trail makes a right angle, turn to the north again; at 1.5 miles and less than fifteen minutes from the fork to North Pond, there is a faint path continuing west. It leads 200 yards across a hogback ridge to a beautiful promontory on the shore of Big Pond. Here you will find several camping spots. On the hemlock knoll you will also find pipsissiwa, shinleaf, and twinflower underfoot.

An alternate western route to the pond begins from Hoffman Road, 0.4 mile west of the road described. Walk a few feet west of the Wilderness Area sign along a power line, then turn right on an old tote road. It heads generally northwest, reaching the western edge of the beaver flow along North Pond's outlet in 0.5 mile.

The old tote road stays in sight of the flow, which is filled with drowned trees. The shores are bordered with blue flag. There are places where you can easily walk to the marsh for good views. The roadway angles west, climbing slightly through a good forest of cedar, hemlock, and white pine. You can see the outlet down below on your right. A 0.8-mile, half-hour walk reaches Big Pond near its outlet. It is a pretty but littered spot.

The path continues west along the shore, but the way is barely discern-

ible. In 0.3 mile it reaches the southwest corner of the pond where there is a good view across the pond to the Blue Ridge Range.

The path continues southwest around a marsh to intersect trails which were used several years ago from Wills Run, then a private cross-country ski area. The trails did continue north, then west to intersect the route from Loch Muller to Big Pond, but portions are so overgrown and flooded that they are currently unusable in any season.

The description of Cole's visit to Big Pond and to North Pond will make you appreciate what trails there are as well as the scenery around both lakes. He wrote, again in his diary:

We now plunged deeper into the woods which were savage. Mouldering giants lay stretched in heaps beneath their surviving descendents. We had some difficulty in finding and forcing our way, and were much annoyed by the mosquitoes which seem to find a congenial home in these dank woods. We heard the sound of falling water and soon got a gleam of silverlight between the mossy trunks—what a scene before and around us—a waveless lake lay at out feet, reflecting perfectly the tall woods that appeared to rise on every hand from its bosom, gigantic and hoary with gray moss that clothed trunks and extended branches and drooped into the waters. Beyond the lake which was perhaps half a mile across rose in an unbroken mass of forest a mountain of pyramidical form—beyond that another of similar form but higher . . . .The mountain heads were reflected in the lake near our feet which trod the shaking and uncertain floor of decaying trees—the trees immediately on the margin of the lake near us were principally the white cedar (arbor vitae). They projected in wild fantastic form far over the lake covered in grisly moss. The day was shadowy, a sombre gloom hung over woods and water adding repose to majesty and on the gray trees shedding a pallid hue, adding seeming death to solitude. The imagination might easily conjure up dread spirits from the deathlike waters—and take the mist that flits among the hoary trees for beings of fearful birth that dwell among the guardians of this dismal lake. But our object was to act and not to indulge in dreamy speculations, but to do either was almost impossible—our tormentors the mosquitoes held headquarters here and from the quaggy shores of the lake had sucked keened poison and sought with ravenous appetite the blood of man. We made some hasty sketches and were glad to retreat covered with sundry blotches and burnings, vowing not to visit again this spot at such a season. This lake may have a name, a Billy or a Roger's . . . but it is worthy of a more poetical one—We thought of several— characteristic Pyramid Lake because of its mountains resembling pyramids— Hoary Lake—Grisly Lake, which latter we thought best although mosquito pond would perhaps have been the most characteristic.

Big Pond Outlet

4 North Pond and Jones Hill
Path, bushwhack, camping, hiking, snowshoeing, map I

From the fork on the path to Big Pond described above, head north for 0.3 mile. Blowdowns obscure the first part of the path, which heads up a slope, but the way soon becomes obvious. This short path takes you briefly uphill, then steeply down to the shore of North Pond. The view alone across North Pond to Hoffman Mountain justifies the trip.

Maps show that a roadway directly from Hoffman Road followed Rogers Brook almost to the outlet of the pond and beyond to the valley west of Jones Hill. Finding this route would mean that you would have a guide to continue around the east end to the pond and north toward Jones Hill. Unfortunately, the road is totally overgrown; however, a bushwhack along that route is still possible. With care you can avoid the marshes in summer and, in winter, on showshoes, you can shorten the trip by crossing both the pond and the marshes. Either way, the views from Jones Hill justify the effort. While traditional approaches to Jones Hill are on private land, this bushwhack is entirely on state land.

Circle to the east of North Pond to its outlet and cross the outlet before it joins Rogers Brook. North of this point, Rogers Brook widens into a wet, marshy, mucky area with no visible open water. Take a course west of north along the eastern side of a small knoll, staying to the west of the marsh. Soon, through the woods, you should see the open water of a shallow pond. The outlet at its southern end is Rogers Brook, which is here, briefly, a narrow, rocky brook. Cross it here.

The shallow pond extends north into the valley west of Jones Hill. Its eastern shore is quite dry and easy to walk along. About two-thirds of the way along the shore take a compass reading on the rocky summit of Jones Hill, which lies approximately to the north-northeast. Head through the dense spruce that border the pond. Very shortly you will emerge in open forest. The way up is along a series of rock slides that face the long southern nose of the mountain. As you climb along that nose, views to the southeast begin.

Continue climbing from one rock patch to another, first enjoying views across the southern end of Schroon Lake and southeast to a surprisingly rocky face of Pharaoh Mountain. Continue climbing and then cross to the west side of the hill for a magnificent view of Hoffman Mountain and Peaked Hills with Dix and Macomb in the High Peaks beyond. Your route to the summit will be a zig-zag from side to side across the ridgeline. The

Edythe Robbins on Jones Hill

summit is a long, thin ridge, rising only to 1830 feet (572 meters), but the views all along it are most impressive.

The path to North Pond is a mile and a quarter long; the bushwhack around the pond and the marshes and up the ridge to the summit is almost two miles long. Allow two and a half to three hours one way for the climb to Jones's summit.

5 East Branch Trout Brook
Path, hiking, camping
3.4 miles one way, 2 hours, 300 feet (94 meters) vertical rise, map I

The overgrown snowmobile trail from North Pond to Loch Muller can be easily followed as far as the East Branch of Trout Brook. Here you will find a lovely place to camp and a charming spot beside the stream for a secluded picnic.

From the eastern route to Big Pond, take the sharp turn to the north described above. It leads west around marshes on the north shore of the pond through a stand of hemlock. T. Morris Longstreth, an early twentieth-century travel writer, made a six-month foot trek through the Adirondacks immediately before World War I. He, too, found pleasure in such a hemlock stand, describing its "soft, bluegreen beauty that lends mystery to its dignity." Even though much of these woods has been logged, they have the timelessness of old woods.

Longstreth wrote:

> The Artist sees a wonderland dripping with shades of green and gray and gold, roofed with spires and domes and black-groined arches, floored with the wildest profusion of ferned rocks and moss-grown trunks. He remembers it fragrant with the damp of twilight, alluring with its glimpses of dim aisles, silent always, always strange. He goes his way.
>
> The camper finds it a spectacle for admiration and for groans. He responds to the fact of its greatness, but finds it not the most useful for his purpose. It is too wet, too large, too empty. But he returns.

This is what you will find on the 1.8 mile, hour-long walk west of Big Pond. You first walk along a ridge with glimpses of the pond, then enjoy the hemlock forest all the way to a stream crossing, here with an intact bridge, 0.6 mile from the pond. There is a short, sharp climb up the following ridge, the very southern end of the Blue Ridge Range. You head briefly down and across a small swampy area and up again. Here yellow birch and maple shelter a stand of maidenhair. The trail continues west over a series of small ridges with only an occasional blowdown or difficult spot until it makes the final descent to a delightful picnic or camping spot on the East Branch.

The continuing route is more bushwhack than path and is described from the trailhead near Loch Muller (section 8).

Irishtown, Loch Muller

THE MAJOR ROUTE west from Schroon Lake was from its southern end near Pottersville on the road that led through Olmstedville toward Minerva. At Olmstedville a track turned north to Irishtown, present County Route 24, circling east to become the Hoffman Road. After the road leaves Olmstedville, it climbs 400 feet before dropping down a hundred feet at the north fork to Loch Muller. The record is not clear on which of the routes early settlers followed to this spot deep in the wilderness—this road through Olmstedville or the Hoffman Road directly from Schroon Lake.

To reach Loch Muller, you can use either approach. From Schroon Lake, drive along Hoffman Road. From the east, Trout Brook Road is a left fork, 4.8 miles from Schroon Lake. One right turn to Loch Muller is .6 mile farther west and a second is 0.8 mile beyond the first turn. From the point the two roads join, 0.9 mile along the eastern spur or 1.3 on the western spur, it is 1.2 miles to a DEC parking area at Loch Muller. The last 0.2 mile is narrow and rutted, downhill across a stream and up to a fork. The way right leads to a large field with ample parking, a view southeast, fireplaces for a picnic, and the two Loch Muller trailheads.

Just before the road makes the descent to the parking area, you pass a large frame building. Stop and read the sign on a huge pine tree, which has been growing since 1833. This is Warren's Hotel, originally a farmhouse which was enlarged into a hotel to make room for hunters and boarders who wished to venture into the northern wilderness.

The hotel register, dating from 1897, tells a tale typical of so many north woods hotels. The building, originally called Bailey Pond Inn, hosted guests who boasted of such feats as this November 15, 1900, entry, "Last day of season—two large does in 2 hours." Trout fishing in nearby ponds was remarkable by modern standards, for visitors in 1901 boasted of a $3\frac{1}{2}$ pound trout; and in 1902 a group from Schroon Lake "caught two trouts in an hour fishing on Marion Pond, one weighing $2\frac{3}{4}$ #, the other $1\frac{3}{4}$ #, total $4\frac{1}{2}$ #." That same year, a group, which included Mrs. Warren, "went to North Branch (205 trout)" while other visitors "fished the pond (40 trout)."

36 Discover the Central Adirondacks

Hunting was good through the 1930s, for a member of a party from Troy "got a 10 pointer, this time on Bailey." George Limebeck, an Essex County guide, shot a ten-point buck in 1938 and remarked, "What a drag from northwest of Marion Pond." But in the early forties, guests and game diminished. In November of 1942 a guestbook entry mused:
> Toast if you wish the girls you've kissed
> But a hunter's toast is to the buck I missed.

Another celebrated the guide:
> With Balsam Fir and spruce by Heck
> You get things done says Old Limebeck.

The last entry in the register is from 1946, which notes "Verry Poor Year— 7 Bucks Killed."

The hotel still stands, a desolate, but handsome frame building. Its register was preserved by neighbors, the Dimmicks; and these entries were taken from a microfilm of the register made by the Adirondack Museum at Blue Mountain Lake.

The property is not posted, but do ask neighbors for permission before walking through the fields north of the hotel. The fields cover the hillside, which drops down to Warren's Pond, where the weed-dappled surface mirrors one of the better views of Hoffman Mountain.

This chapter takes you to ponds visited by the hotel's guests, the same ones that the D&H Guide for 1907 advertised as available to guests from Bailey Pond Inn: "Five other ponds stocked with bass, two with pickerel, two with trout. Pure Mountain air. No better hunting grounds. Accomodates 25. Terms $8 to $12 per week."

Hoffman Notch

6 The Split Glacial Erratic
Bushwhack, map I

The geological survey for the Schroon Lake quadrangle contains a photograph of a huge glacial erratic perched on the side of a hill in a field. It is just one of the many boulders of Marcy anorthosite which the glaciers swept from the High Peaks region and deposited miles from their origins. You will find impressive giants throughout the Hoffman Notch area.

The caption on the photograph in the survey describes the location of the split erratic as "near the base of Cobble Hill three-fourths of a mile southwest of Warren's Hotel. It is approximately 33 feet long, 27 feet wide, and 25 feet high." It is likely that in 1919 when the survey was published, there were fields all the way from the hotel to the erratic. Finding it today is not so easy; but for the curious, it is a different sort of a short excursion.

A dirt road leads to the west from the road to Loch Muller, 0.3 mile south of Warren's Hotel. It leads past several homes but ends at the edge of state land in a circle through a field with abandoned cars. At the northwest side of the circle there is a path heading downhill following an old tote road. Its beginning is concealed in tall weeds beside a dying maple.

The tote road becomes obvious as soon as it leaves the field. It crosses an intermittent stream and heads west, winding uphill. As the roadway

approaches the height of land and begins to curve to the right at a point marked by a giant spruce, leave the track and head west and contour around the hillside. When you reach an open patch with bracken, about five minutes from the track, turn southwest, left, and downhill. Within 100 feet you should see the boulder in the woods to your right. It is perched against the hillside and appears much dwarfed by surrounding trees.

Total time for the bushwhack is less than an hour. The tote road continues but gradually disappears. Its disappearance is unfortunate because it once led to an old trail which led from Loch Muller to Minerva Stream (section 65) and on west to Green Mountain, allowing workers from the Loch Muller area to reach the iron mine there (section 19).

7 Loch Muller to Big Marsh at Hoffman Notch

Marked trail, ski touring, hiking
4 miles to Big Marsh, 2½ hours one way, 100 feet plus several small rises; this is part of a through trip, 7.6 miles to the Blue Ridge Road (section 70), 6 hours one way, map I

From the DEC parking area at Loch Muller, take the yellow trail from the north edge of the lot. The trail follows an old tote road and generally heads

Views across Big Marsh toward Hoffman Mountain

downhill, contouring to the northwest. Within five minutes, a quarter mile, you cross the outlet of Bailey Pond on an impressive new bridge. The roadway takes a gentle uphill course through scrubby reforestation and second growth.

As the trail descends, you cross a second stream, this one a small drainage from the slopes of Washburn Ridge. The trail takes an easterly direction at a second rise, then heads downhill. From here on the forest cover is what you expect of the Hoffman Notch Wilderness—lovely woods with mature trees that have been growing for a century or more.

The trail crosses a third small stream and turns to follow it. There are several blowdowns across the trail, which nevertheless remains very easy to follow. You reach the border of wet bottom land after a forty-minute, 1.4-mile walk, and approach the North Branch of Trout Brook.

Here the trail turns north and follows the brook 2.6 miles to Big Marsh. The climb into the valley of the notch is gradual though the stream drops enough to create cascades all along the brook. The brook is pinched between the steep flanks of Washburn and Texas ridges and filled with giant boulders and erratics. The forest of maple, yellow birch, and hemlock darkens the valley and makes it a moist place for ferns and mosses. The stump of one forest giant, a yellow birch, measures more than twelve feet in circumference. Several live trees in the valley measure nearly eleven feet.

You are close to the stream except where the trail swings briefly west around a small glacial drumlin. The trail weaves between piles of boulders and the ledges of Washburn Ridge. You cross a number of small streams that drain that ridge.

At 2.4 miles the trail reaches a marshy area bordered by tall spruce, and the valley becomes wider. You can now see the outline of Texas Ridge across the flow, which is filling with the sphagnum mat of a typical bog. Five minutes later, you pass a second marsh, then a third, which is now only a dry grassy meadow with a beaver dam that no longer holds water. You follow the 1.5-mile chain of marshes for nearly forty minutes. Then the valley narrows again, and the trail climbs over a small knoll and passes several small ledges as it threads its way past more boulders and erratics.

The valley opens up again into Big Marsh, an open flow of shallow water that mirrors Texas Ridge. The trail along the marsh weaves past more boulders and ledges. Here the steep slopes of Washburn Ridge descend precipitously to the west side of the marsh. You can find a good boulder about halfway along the marsh for a dry picnic perch. After a quiet contemplation of the western slopes of the Blue Ridge Range, you can either return to Loch Muller or continue on the through trip to the Blue Ridge Road.

8 Loch Muller to Big Pond
Bushwhack, hiking, snowshoeing, map I

It seems incongruous to call a route whose beginning and ending are the well-marked trails described above and in sections 5 and 7 a bushwhack, but it is nevertheless a bushwack and a miserable one at present. The entire 7-mile route was marked out as a snowmobile trail before the area was declared a Wilderness, that is, before 1972. For several years after that, skiers used this route because it is a great wilderness trek. But, you will be amazed at the way the forest can conceal a route that is not much used and never cleared. Because of the blowdowns, you could not ski it now, even if you could find the route. But you might attempt it on snowshoes; and, with a compass and a good imagination, it is possible to follow the overgrown middle 2.2-mile section as a hiking route.

Where the trail from Loch Muller to Big Marsh first approaches the North Branch of Trout Brook at 1.4 miles, turn east from the trail and you will find the decaying snowmobile bridge concealed by tall weeds. On the far side of the bridge, the trail, marked with blue hiking disks and an occasional orange snowmobile disk which no one saw fit to remove, turns uphill, fairly steeply, on an easterly bearing, then turns generally southeast. As the trail levels out, the route, with patches of corduroy in the wet ferny areas and all the other signs of having once been a tote road, takes a southerly course.

As the trail continues uphill, east of south, you will find the way blocked by dense stands of witch hobble. The route does not improve where the trail heads downhill (perhaps it should be called an old trail, like an old road, to distinguish it from ones that are currently marked). Forty-five minutes and about a mile and a half from the bridge, the trail turns almost south again and crosses a hemlock ridge which is a deer-yarding area in winter.

The way east of the hemlock ridge is hard to find. The growth in the trail becomes so thick that you feel as if the thicker it is, the more certain you are that you are on course. There are still trail-marking disks along the way. Another clue to the trail is the ends of sawed logs which were once cleared from it.

You now contour around the hill taking an easterly course again. Between two intermittent streams there is an open area where you may sense a track heading south. You bear left into the thickest growth, where blowdowns have made an enormous mess of the trail. Suddenly the trail shifts to a course of north of east as it continues contouring around the slopes of Texas Ridge, and you reach the East Branch.

No signs of the old tote road, which led north along the East Branch, can be found; but if you enjoy bushwhacking, head north along either the East Branch or its tributary from Buck Hollow. I am told there is a beautiful waterfall somewhere up here along one of these two streams, which drop from deep clefts between Texas Ridge and the Blue Ridge.

9 Bailey Pond
Marked trail, walking, camping, skiing
1 mile one way, ½ hour, minimal vertical rise, map I

A blue-marked trail begins from the DEC parking lot north of Loch Muller. It starts to the left, west of the yellow trail to Big Marsh, circles for 200 yards behind private land, and intersects the roadway that originally led directly from Warren's Hotel to Bailey Pond. The road and its continuation make a great ski-touring route.

The mile-long roadway is straight and level. Within sight of the outlet the trail turns west for 100 yards to the marshy outlet of the pond. There is a stone foundation near the outlet and rocks, indicating there once might have been a dam. Most of the shoreline is marshy. The view west across the pond to Hayes Mountain is very handsome.

10 Bailey Pond Inlet and Marion Pond
Paths, skiing, hiking, fishing, maps I, III

The walk to Bailey Pond from the Loch Muller Parking Area is so short you will certainly want to extend it as far as the end of the old road at the site of two dwellings 1.2 miles north of the pond. The roadway is so obvious it needs no description except to tempt you to follow it by hinting that you will enjoy views of the gorge that surrounds Bailey Pond Inlet.

The roadway crosses the inlet after half a mile at a bridge that is still intact and continues close to the gorge. Just after the road crosses a small stream, the outlet of Marion Pond, the road seems to disappear at the edge of a coniferous swamp.

Marion Pond sits high on the southern slopes of Hayes Mountain. It takes a bit of searching to find the beginning of the path to it. The path is a traditional fishermen's path, overgrown in places, obvious to those who have walked it before.

At the road's apparent end, head briefly north, then northwest, up the steep slopes. There are traces of paths which join into one relatively distinct route in 200 yards and the path becomes quite obvious as the course turns to the southwest to traverse the hillside. The route then stays generally west and there are places where you can lose it. The course levels out and approaches a wall of hillside where it turns almost north to circle around the steep ridge. As the path completes the circle to resume its south-southwest course, it heads up through a draw. Here maple and beech starts are filling in a blowdown area and cover the path.

At the head of the draw, the path makes a sharp turn to the right and abruptly uphill. This spot is exceedingly tricky on the return so mark it well. At the top of the short rise—200 yards—the path turns south again. After a sharp left, an angle to the right leads you up a ridge. Here more dense maples and beech obscure the way. Finally you enter a trough, a long draw, that leads to the pond, but your final approach to the pond is along the ridge which forms the east side of the draw.

For all this contorted description, it takes no more than thirty minutes to walk the 1.2-mile path to the pond. For some reason, the path appears less obvious on the way down, and you can easily spend a quarter hour more just looking for the route.

Solitude and quiet greet you at the pond, which is very tiny. A small camping area is at the end of the path beside the pond.

11 Bailey Pond Inlet to Washburn Ridge
Bushwhack, map I

The road along Bailey Pond Inlet does not really end as described above; it is merely so difficult to follow that any continuing route must be called a bushwhack. In any event, you might want to go farther than the roadway ever did and make your way along the west face of Washburn Ridge to a point southwest of Big Marsh, where ledges offer a view northwest across Durgin Brook Valley and the Blue Ridge Road.

From the "end" of the road, head north through the coniferous swamp and angle right toward the inlet stream. Walk along it until you find the remains of an old bridge across it. You can follow the stream or the road where it is not overgrown for about 0.5 mile. Then the roadway leaves the stream, continuing north for another 0.3 mile until it makes a sharp right

turn to climb the ridge via a draw. You will be amazed to find old wooden culverts, old bridges, washed-out areas, and signs that the road was built up by a fairly substantial rock base in places.

The roadway virtually disappears as it swings southeast at the head of the draw at about the 2400-foot (750-meter) level. Here you can begin a bushwhack along the ridge searching for cliffs, which are about 100 feet higher.

There is a very handsome marsh at the head of the valley. The northern end of the marsh is the headwaters of Durgin Brook, and the marsh is squeezed between the steep slopes of Bailey Hill and Washburn Ridge.

If you make the trip on a warm summer day, leave the roadway and slide down the steep slopes of the ridge to the inlet to follow it down to the old bridge. Along the way you will find pools in which to cool off and many glittering, little cascades. The inlet drops 400 feet between the marshes and the road; most of the drop is in the deepest part of the gorge, which is less than half a mile long.

12 The 1808 Hoffman Cemetery
Short walk or cross-country ski trip, map I

About 30 feet east of the turn from Hoffman Road to the western road to Loch Muller, an old road leads southwest into the woods. It is a pleasant twenty-minute walk to the 1808 cemetery along the road bordered by tall white pines.

Park at the edge of Hoffman Road, for the way to the cemetery is along a typical old road that today is best for walking. After a five-minute walk you reach the outlet of Muller Pond, a tributary of Trout Brook. You cross the outlet on a small but sound footbridge which replaces a larger span that has collapsed.

Beyond the outlet the old road heads uphill through dense pine forests that give way to mixed hardwoods. Fifteen minutes, 0.6 mile, from the highway, the roadway turns abruptly right, west; and from here it is 200 yards to a small clearing which holds the cemetery.

The graveyard, which is nestled in the clearing, is partially enveloped by the spreading branches of two huge pines. Names on the thirty to forty graves reflect the early settlers, many from the Oliver family; and several have flags indicating Civil War veterans. Reading the inscriptions and

Bailey Pond

noting the young age at which many died, you will sense the hardships experienced by this early Adirondack community.

The cemetery, now so deep in the woods, was actually just off the original road from Loch Muller to Irishtown. The way west beyond the cemetery is heavily overgrown but intersects Hoffman Road opposite Oliver Pond. If you choose to ski to the cemetery, the downhill return run from the cemetery to Hoffman Road takes less than ten minutes.

13 Muller Pond
Camping, fishing, map I

Several good campsites lie between Hoffman Road and Muller Pond, a very short distance from the road in evergreen stands on the dry northeastern corner of the pond. The western shore is marshy. You can easily get a boat or canoe to the pond to explore its 0.4-mile length and its pine- and spruce-covered island.

Dirt tracks head south from the Hoffman Road, 0.4 mile west of the western road to Loch Muller. The pond, which lies entirely on state land, is but 200 yards from the road.

14 Oliver Pond
Camping, picnicking, map I

Both ends of marshy Oliver Pond are right off Hoffman Road and both accesses are on state land. Plan to stop at either one for a picnic here and be sure to bring a canoe to explore the marshes of the 0.5 mile long pond. You can delight in its birds, wild flowers, mats of waterlilies, twisted stumps, and reflections.

The dirt road turnoff to the northern end of the pond is 1.4 miles southwest of the western road to Loch Muller. It leads 100 yards to several campsites and an easy canoe launch site. The southern end is 0.5 south by road or 2.7 miles north of Irishtown (4.6 miles north of Olmstedville). A picnic site not far from the road is in a deep hemlock grove overlooking the marsh, but access to the pond is not so good as at the northern end.

North Creek to Tahawus—The Roosevelt Memorial Highway

PARTS OF THE road from North Creek to Tahawus and Newcomb have a venerable history; parts are remarkably recent additions. NY 28 N will be your guide to history as well as hiking.

The first bridge over the Hudson at North Creek was not constructed until 1875; its modern successor was built in 1929. NY 28 N was first surfaced in 1908. But Minerva, 7 miles north of North Creek, was settled long before, starting as early as 1800. The town was on the Chester to Canton Road (1808), whose precise original route is unclear.

Originally part of the Totten and Crossfield Patent, the land to the north of Minerva Township was divided into three patents in 1786. Francis Dominick's 12,000 acres were surveyed into lots in 1798 by Robert Moxham, for whom Moxham Mountain and Pond were named.

Settlers came early in the nineteenth century to harvest timber and carve out farms. There was enough traffic on the road from Minerva to Newcomb that several guest houses were built along the route, the most famous of which was Aiden Lair built by Sheldon Hewitt after 1857. A succession of hostelers enlarged the enterprise, attracting visitors to the nearby trout streams and good hunting. One Scots guest named the place Aiden Lair, meaning haven of rest. A three-story lodge, built in 1893 by Michael Cronin, burned in 1914. This was replaced on the opposite side of the road by the current building, which now has a historical marker.

North of Aiden Lair, the road passes through a large tract of state land which borders the road for six miles. The tract was acquired by the state for defaulted taxes in 1877; and, although some of it burned, forest recovery was well under way by the turn of the century.

48 Discover the Central Adirondacks

All the stories of early travelers are overshadowed by the events of the night of September 13, 1901—events that began when then Vice President Theodore Roosevelt learned, on his descent from a climb up Mount Marcy, that President McKinley had been shot. Roosevelt completed the long descent by late afternoon, and arrangements were made to leave for North Creek at the first light next day. News of McKinley's worsening condition made Roosevelt decide to leave that night, against all advice and reason, given the dangers of a horsedrawn cart on the dark and dangerously rutted road. His mad forty-mile dash in three relays took him, in just over five hours, to the railhead at North Creek. A memorial stone beside the highway south of the Tahawus junction marks the approximate place he would have passed at the moment when McKinley died.

15 Moxham Mountain
Bushwhack, map II

The drive north from the Hudson is dominated by views of Moxham Mountain with its tremendous rock faces. Moxham is a series of peaks resembling a closed, left fist, with gentle northern slopes and steep southern faces, rising to the western peak, which is Moxham's summit. (The summit was originally named Mount Jones.) The mountain is entirely surrounded by private lands though at least one of the property owners does not mind people crossing to gain access to state lands on the north face. Obey all No Trespassing signs, however.

Fourteenth Road was the main road west from Minerva, surveyed in 1826 as far as Deer Creek and down to a ford crossing of the Hudson at North River two years later. This road, site of many early farms, has a number of private homes; but a mile beyond Deer Creek crossing, the road enters state land. You can walk along this stretch of road but can no longer use it to reach the Hudson. To reach the public stretch, drive west on Fourteenth Road for 1.4 miles; then take the right fork. Continue for nearly 2 more miles to the bridge over Deer Creek where the road turns left. The road follows Deer Creek downstream for 1.2 miles to state land. Taking a left fork and walking beyond this point, you are sometimes close enough to Deer Creek to enjoy its small falls as the road gradually descends to posted land at river level. This 1.5-mile stretch is a quiet road for a secluded walk.

View South from Moxham

50   Discover the Central Adirondacks

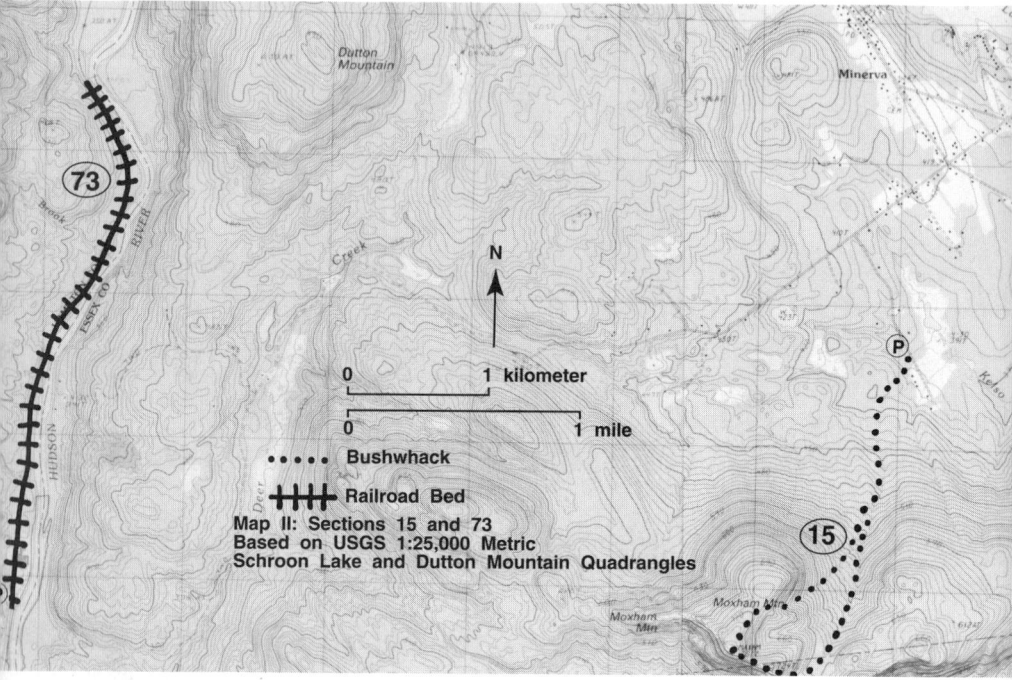

Fourteenth Road will also start you on your climb of Moxham Mountain. There are no marked trails; but the area is hunted extensively, and a path of sorts can be followed to start you on the way toward the summit. Turn left from Fourteenth Lake Road 0.6 mile west of Minerva and follow McKee Road south for 0.6 mile to a dirt track on the right. The first of two trailers on McKee Road is just beyond the dirt track. The trip starts on the track on private land, which currently can be crossed without specific permission.

Follow the dirt track uphill. Shortly a stream appears on your left. In ten minutes you pass a hunting camp; continue on the track, taking a right fork at an old log staging area. Take a second right fork; then at a V, go left, heading generally south as the track fades. Continue south, now following a compass route though there is a small stream just to the east at this point, which can serve as a guide.

Within thirty minutes from the start, you reach state land. The forest of tall hardwoods, open beneath, is the clue. Angling west of south beside the stream, your climb is steady; and in less than thirty minutes more, you

Moxham Mountain

approach a cliff. Climb beneath the eastern flanks of the cliff and head west up the steep ledges to a knob; then continue south on a nearly flat ridge. The cover becomes denser, and the way slightly steeper as you approach the summit ridge. Two hours are more than enough for the ascent.

Follow open rock to the 2400-foot (751-meter) western summit with its spectacular views of Vanderwhacker, Santanoni, Blue Mountain, Casey, Snowy, Bullhead and Puffer, Gore, the north flanks of the small mountains that line the East Branch of the Sacandaga, and, in the distant south, Crane and Huckleberry. Closer in you see the town of North Creek and the Hudson River. Before you head back, walk east along the summit ridge to the next intriguing knob in the chain. There are lovely views of the four little ponds below the cliffs. More knobs to the east beckon. If you head into the draw east of the knob, carefully pick a compass course to the north. It leads through a saddle and down into a draw that seems to funnel you. You will be surprised at how easily it returns you to the dirt tracks for the final descent.

16 Stony, Big and Little Sherman Ponds, and Falls Brook to Irishtown

Snowmobile trail, hiking, camping, good cross-country skiing
5.8 miles, 3½ hours, many small rises and 900 foot descent, map III

Measure the points along NY 28 N from the intersection of County Route 30 south of the post office in Minerva. It is exactly 2 miles north from here to the turnoff on the left, west, to the North Woods Club Road (next chapter) and 3.8 miles to the trailhead, on the right, for Stony Pond.

The best way to enjoy this trail, unless you are planning to camp at one of the interior ponds, is on a through trip with a second car spotted at John Brannon Road, 0.3 mile north of the landfill in Irishtown. There is plenty along the way to stretch this to a full day's outing.

This marked snowmobile trail follows an old road 2 miles to Stony Pond with its lean-to. Five minutes into the walk, notice a right fork which leads in 200 yards to a high camping spot on the state land shore of Twenty-ninth Pond. The left fork, the main trail, continues uphill and reaches a height-of-land within another five minutes. Ten minutes later the trail crosses an intermittent stream with a large wetland visible off to the right. A beaver dam on the stream to the left of the trail barely keeps the trail dry. The trail climbs again, then descends to a second beaver flow and continues along the outlet of the pond to the lean-to.

It takes no more than forty minutes to reach the pond with its spruce-covered shoreline, dominated by Green Mountain to the east. A sign points right, south, 4 miles to Irishtown; it is actually 3.8 miles to trailhead on John Brannon Road. The trail swings uphill away from the pond, descending to pond level at a small marsh beneath a vertical rock face. Beaver flooding has overflowed a natural spring beneath the ledge and forces you to detour around the marsh right beneath the ledge. This rock face might be fun to scale with ropes. Red trail markers join the orange snowmobile trail disks to help you on the detour.

You climb a small ridge. The height-of-land here might be a good beginning point for a bushwhack east up Green Mountain, which has several ranges of inviting cliffs. Beyond the ridge, the trail drops through a draw to the Sherman Ponds, a half-hour, 0.8-mile walk if you stop for photographs at the marsh.

Old maps are most confusing here. There once was a roadway leading

Stony Pond Lean-to

north to Center Pond (section 19). This route is so overgrown that no sign of it can be found. The through road, which the trail generally follows, used to cross a causeway between the Sherman Ponds and continue south on the east side of Big Sherman. Beavers have changed all that; now a narrow foot trail has been cut along the west side of Big Sherman, back from the pond, climbing up and over rises between two bays and another rise between the southern bay and the outlet. The outlet is in such a narrow draw that only a very small beaver dam is needed to raise the water level and flood a large stand of spruce and hemlock now starkly guarding the outlet. That same small rise in water level accounts for the flooding of the old causeway between the two ponds.

The trail crosses the outlet gorge 1.5 miles from Stony Pond Lean-to; and on the west side of the gorge, traces of the old roadway are visible, leading to camping places. The trail continues south, then east through a beautiful deciduous forest of maple and ash. The trail crosses two yellow-marked property lines; and, beyond the second, the trail is quite close to the site of an iron mine, which opened about 1869 and closed in 1881 as the Burden Iron Company. During this period several open pits were worked on the hillside to the north, but most had filled with rubble at the time the *Geology of the Schroon Lake Quadrangle,* New York State Museum Bulletin, was written by William J. Miller in 1919. The pits and trenches extended along a vein 500 yards long.

Ore from this mine was taken down the road the trail now follows to the Minerva Iron Company, whose forge with eight fires was built in 1869. However, this iron company failed, and the last ore from the mine was shipped to Troy about 1880.

The trail continues southeast down the flanks of Green Mountain, formerly called Ore Bed Mountain. A big draw opens to the left; then the trail ascends a small ridge. The next section of broad open trail is a delight to walk—with trail and trailside filled with stands of maidenhair, marsh, and rattlesnake ferns beneath a tall canopy of imposing, straight-trunked, mixed deciduous trees.

Just over 2 miles from the outlet of Sherman Pond, you cross a boundary marking the end of state land. Then the trail approaches Falls Brook (as Sherman Pond's outlet stream is called). For a short distance, the trail accompanies the brook with its smooth bedrock base, covered by a hemlock canopy. After the trail crosses the brook near a small falls, it quickly reaches Long Hill Road.

17 Rankin Pond

Marked trail, short walk, camping, fishing, map III

Many of the lakes and ponds close to NY 28 N are privately owned; and the largest, Balfour Lake, has both a girls' and a boys' camp. One tear-drop of a pond is entirely state owned and can be reached in ten minutes from the highway. The trailhead is 200 yards north of the Stony Pond trailhead on the west side of the road. An abandoned roadway leads north toward Balfour Lake. The trail, blue-marked, is almost hidden to the left, south, of the roadway, within 50 feet of the highway.

The short, 0.3 mile trail descends through a hemlock-covered draw to the pond, crossing two wet places and some blowdowns on the way. Crusher Hill drops sharply to pond side on the east, and Rankin Pond Mountain rises over 300 feet above the pond to the north; but most of the pond's western shores are marshy.

18 Hewitt Pond
Marked trail, fishing, camping, skiing
0.6 mile, 15 minutes, map III

The west end of Hewitt Pond is privately owned, but the entire eastern end is state land. The trail is designed to avoid the pond and lead the hiker on to other adventures (see next section). The reason the trail was designed this way has, of course, a historical origin.

Collins Hewitt moved to Minerva from the Pendletown settlement, later Newcomb, in 1819 with his six sons. His son Sheldon wanted nothing more than to be a mighty hunter, living, trapping, fishing in the wild. He built a hunting cabin on the west shore of the pond—now named for him—and guided many people to places in the north woods. Among those he guided was John Burroughs, who described besting Hewitt in fishing near his camp on the Stillwater on the Boreas (section 26).

Sheldon Hewitt had seven children; his oldest daughter Jane married Daniel Gates, and they ran the original guest house west of Aiden Lair.

Burroughs' writing inspired Sarah M. Sage, wife of a prominent Albany businessman, to find the kind of secluded Adirondack spot Burroughs described. The Hewitt Pond property suited her perfectly. Just before the turn of the century a camp was built, followed by others for the family's children. The family turned the property into a private conservation park under the state's Forest, Fish, and Game Law. In 1910 family members incorporated the property into the Hewitt Pond Club, which survives to this day.

Sometime before the turn of the century, Michael Cronin, the proprietor of Aiden Lair, cut the trail which circles around private lands to the state-owned side. The route, starting out through a spruce swamp, is now part of the state-marked trail, complete with many lengths of boardwalk to keep hikers dry.

The Hewitt Pond Club Road is 5 miles north of the North Woods Club Road. Drive east along it for 0.5 mile to a parking area, adjacent to the gate to the club property. The trail, with red markers, heads east through the swamp, with labrador tea and lady's slippers bordering the boardwalk. Here and at a marsh along the access road, you may spot a Canada jay.

The trail climbs up a small hill to the south of the pond, staying just south of the private property. It descends from the hill to reach the shore in a bay where fishermen often keep boats. The shore east of here is all Forest Preserve. The trail briefly follows the shore of the bay and at 0.6

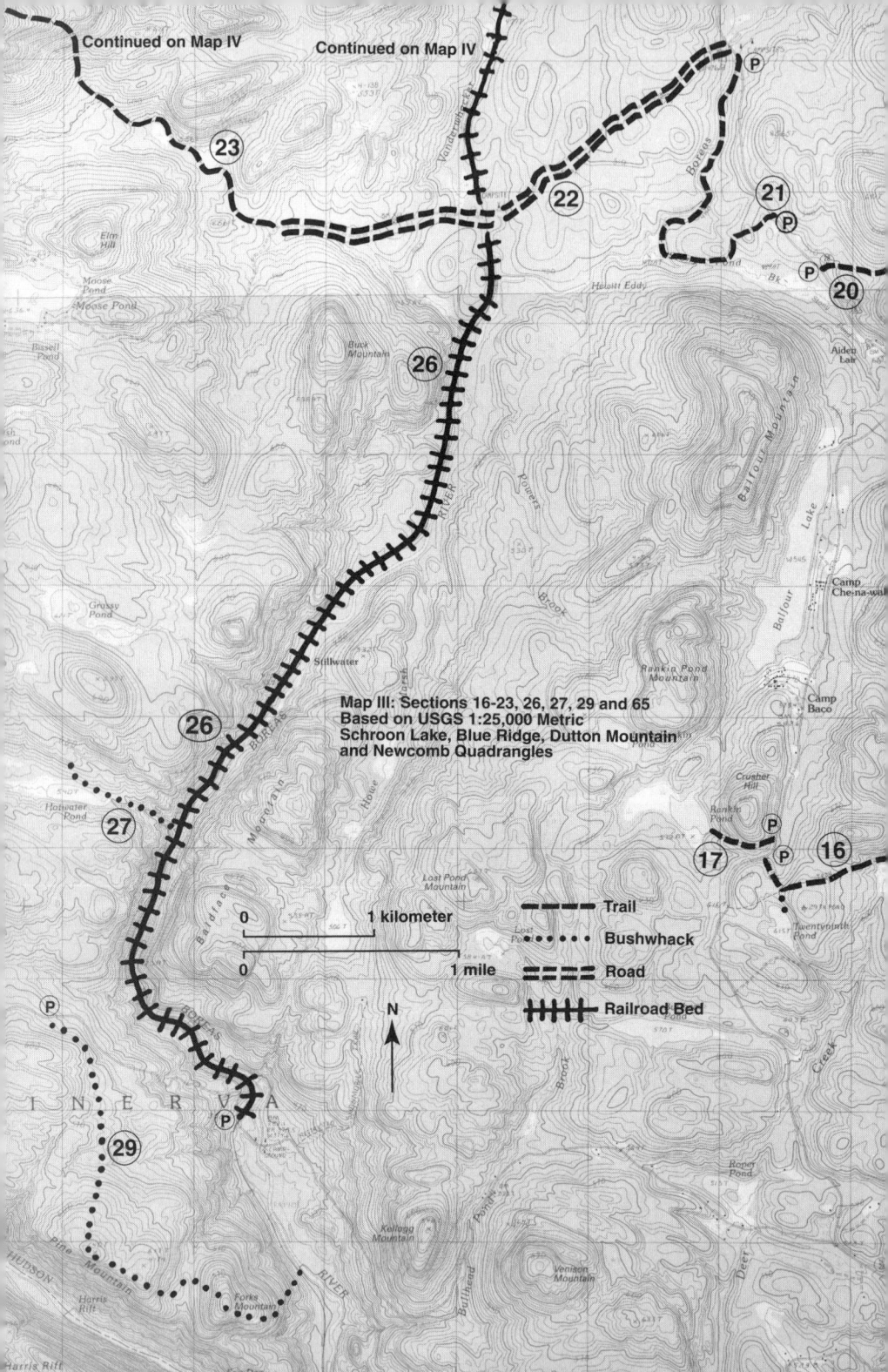

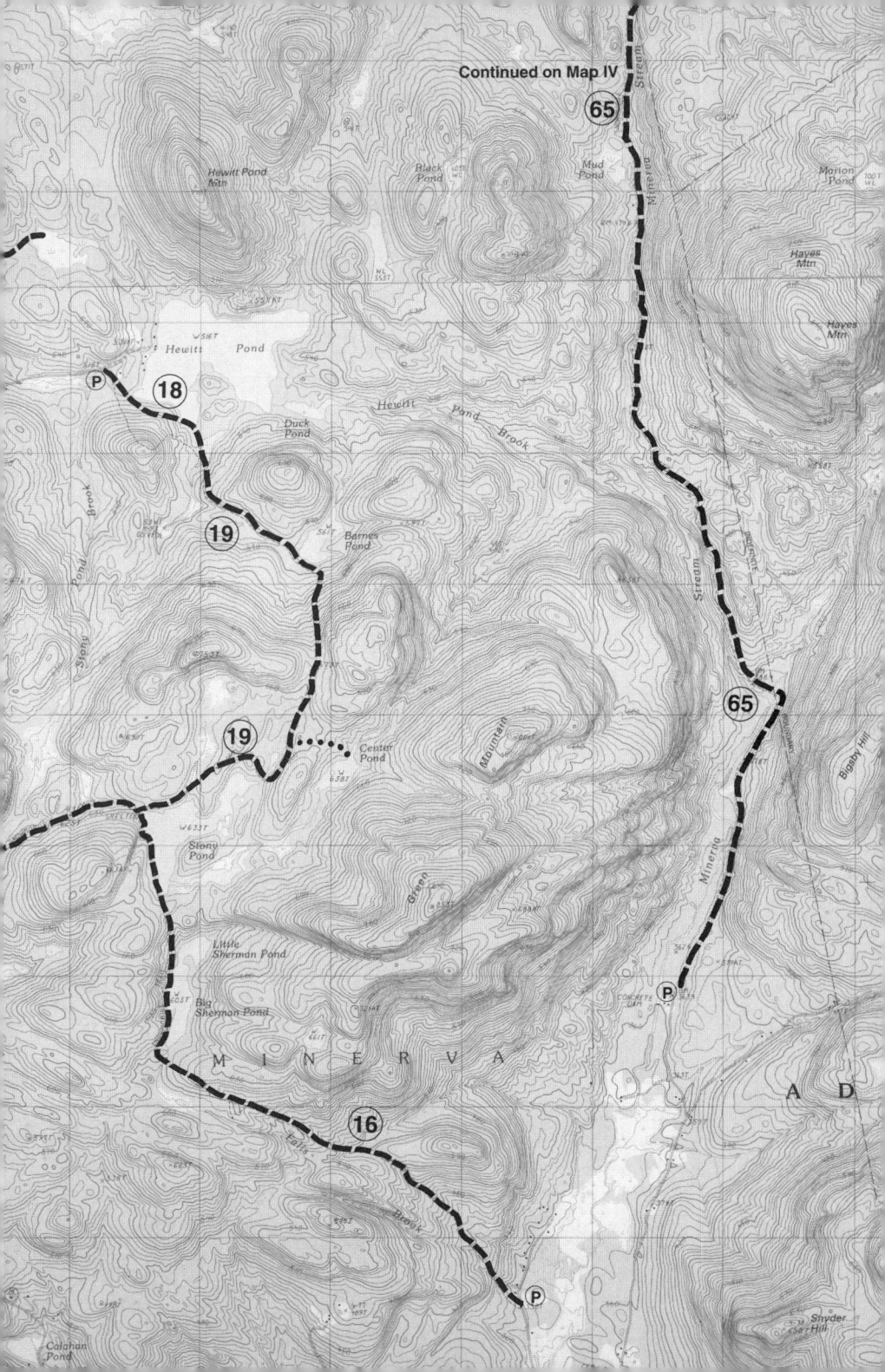

mile crosses an inlet and leaves the shore to head uphill away from the pond at the point a peninsula juts north into the pond. There are several faint paths in this vicinity, all heading north and east to the pond, all used by sportsmen to reach the Forest Preserve portions of the shoreline. Beyond the peninsula is a marsh area known as Duck Pond, but the rest of the shoreline is fairly high and dry. Views from the peninsula are across to Hewitt Pond Mountain. Note that the Club lands extend over half the pond, all of the western end; and fishing there is prohibited.

19 Hewitt, Barnes, Center, and Stony Ponds Circuit

Marked trail, hiking, fishing, skiing, camping
5.6-mile circuit, 0.3-mile spur, 3½ hours, 300 feet (94 meters) vertical rise, map III

A delightful circuit is traced by the marked state trails connecting these four ponds. The route makes a good ski trip as well as a good hiking trip. With cars at either end, Stony Pond (section 16) and Hewitt Pond (above) the through route is possible. The trails are described from north to south, but the reverse is equally appropriate.

After making the fifteen-minute walk to the shore of Hewitt Pond, continue following the trail as it crosses the inlet and heads south, then south of east, uphill, passing a small marsh that is to the right of the trail. The route is a gentle uphill, through a saddle, then a brief descent to Barnes Pond, 1.6 miles from the trailhead, a thirty-five-minute walk.

The trail hugs the shore of Barnes Pond with its stark, dead trunks and old beaver work, for 200 yards, then leaves the pond to head uphill at 190° magnetic on a beautifully forested hillside.

As the route becomes steeper, the trail angles to east of south heading through a draw. The trail is obviously following an old tote road whose open course is all too readily filled with brushy maple starts. At 2.2 miles, twenty minutes and 0.6 mile from Barnes Pond, the trail reaches a height-of-land. A developing drainage which has joined the tote road angles right, but the trail stays left. It is a tricky place, and the continuing trail, still following the tote road, is poorly drained with washes on both sides.

A marsh develops to the right of the trail at 2.5 miles. This turns into open water, a beaver flow not shown on the USGS maps. The trail follows

Stony Pond

the east side of the flow, generally back from it, cut within a decade or so along a course through dense spruce and balsam thickets. After walking along the flow for a few minutes, begin to watch for a trail junction. One mile from Barnes Pond, a yellow marker leads you east on a narrow footpath uphill through a draw and down to Center Pond. This new route appears rarely walked, but the trail is fairly clear. This side trail reaches Center Pond in 0.3 mile, a ten-minute walk.

There is a camping spot at the pond, which is buggy, wet, and full of stumps with a small, spruce-covered island on the west side. The scene is typically north woods. The quality of the fishing is not known, but the site is as remote as you could wish.

Return to the red trail and head south, briefly beside the flow, then along the outlet of the flow. The trail turns and crosses the small stream. Here you might wish to leave the trail to continue parallel to the outlet which reaches an arm of Stony Pond after 100 dense yards.

Beyond the stream crossing, the trail winds west, over a ridge and back down to pond level. You make a wet crossing of a marshy drainage that is flowing into Stony Pond. The trail is again obviously following the tote road and is barely within sight of the pond. A thirty-minute walk, 1 mile from the yellow trail junction, the red trail reaches the outlet of Stony Pond. You have to improvise a crossing on logs and rocks, most easily done a bit downstream from the trail if water is high. You are within sight of the lean-to on Stony and 2 miles from NY 28 N via the Stony Pond trail.

20 Lindsey Marsh

Marked trail, snowshoeing, cross-country skiing
1.5 miles, relatively level, 45 minutes, maps III, IV

The trail to Lindsey Marsh is an enigma. It really does not lead to anything spectacular or easy to appreciate. In spite of a couple of blowdowns, this is an excellent cross-country ski trail and being able to explore the huge marsh on skis would be fun. Since winter is the best time to visit Lindsey Marsh, you could also try this route on showshoes. In summer there is really no way to enjoy the spruce- and balsam-ringed shoreline or find the botanical gems in the marsh.

The trail is 1.1 miles south of the NY 28 N bridge over the Boreas, 5.4 miles north of the North Woods Club Road. It is marked with yellow trail markers and occasional snowmobile disks even though the route is not currently a designated snowmobile trail. The trailhead sign says 2.5 miles to the marsh; it is more like 1.5 miles, at most a forty-five-minute walk.

East of the trailhead, you pass a log landing and a foundation and cross a very small stream twice. After the short rise, the forest becomes more open, taller, more handsome. The trail makes a long arc around a hillside, heading generally east. Beyond a new log bridge the trail goes through a pine stand, up a hill into a lovely hardwood stand, and across a second pine knoll. The tall canopy continues with open understory, making it easy to see ahead as the trail descends to the dense spruce thickets that edge the marsh.

The marsh is also bordered with leatherleaf, labrador tea, winterberry, bunchberry, lady's slippers in great profusion, and mounds of the fragrant Linnaen twinflower. Tamarack dot the marsh. If you can stand the bugs, the late spring-early summer plants are marvelous. If you make the trip in winter, strike out south, then east to explore the far reaches of the marsh and enjoy an extra hour of skiing.

21 Boreas Circuit

Marked trail, short walk, swimming, picnicking
2 miles, 1 hour plus, minimal elevation change, maps III, IV

Few trails this short are as pleasant as the loop that begins 0.25 mile north of the Lindsey Marsh Trail and loops back to NY 28 N by the bridge over the Boreas. The southern guideboard gives the distance to Hewitt Eddy on the Boreas as 0.75 mile, to NY 28 N as 2 miles.

The trail roughly parallels the outlet of Hewitt Pond, out of sight of it. It is a charming narrow footpath with pine needles underfoot from the scattered large pine, sphagnum in the wet areas beneath the spruce. In 0.5 mile, the trail approaches a tiny stream, which is the outlet of Stony Pond, follows it briefly, then plunges over a dense spruce-covered knoll. A small swamp follows; then the Boreas appears. Hewitt Eddy is downstream, and there is a small but beautiful waterfall upstream on the Boreas.

The trail turns north to follow the Boreas on ledges above the river. You should pause for a photograph by the falls. A camping spot nearby is sheltered by beautiful tall trees. Further north, the Boreas flows through a little gorge. At the deep pool upstream, look for the iron bolt and ring fixed in the bedrock. This spot, immediately below the stillwater, was the site of a log boom which restrained logs until water conditions permitted them to be run through the rapids dowstream to the Hudson.

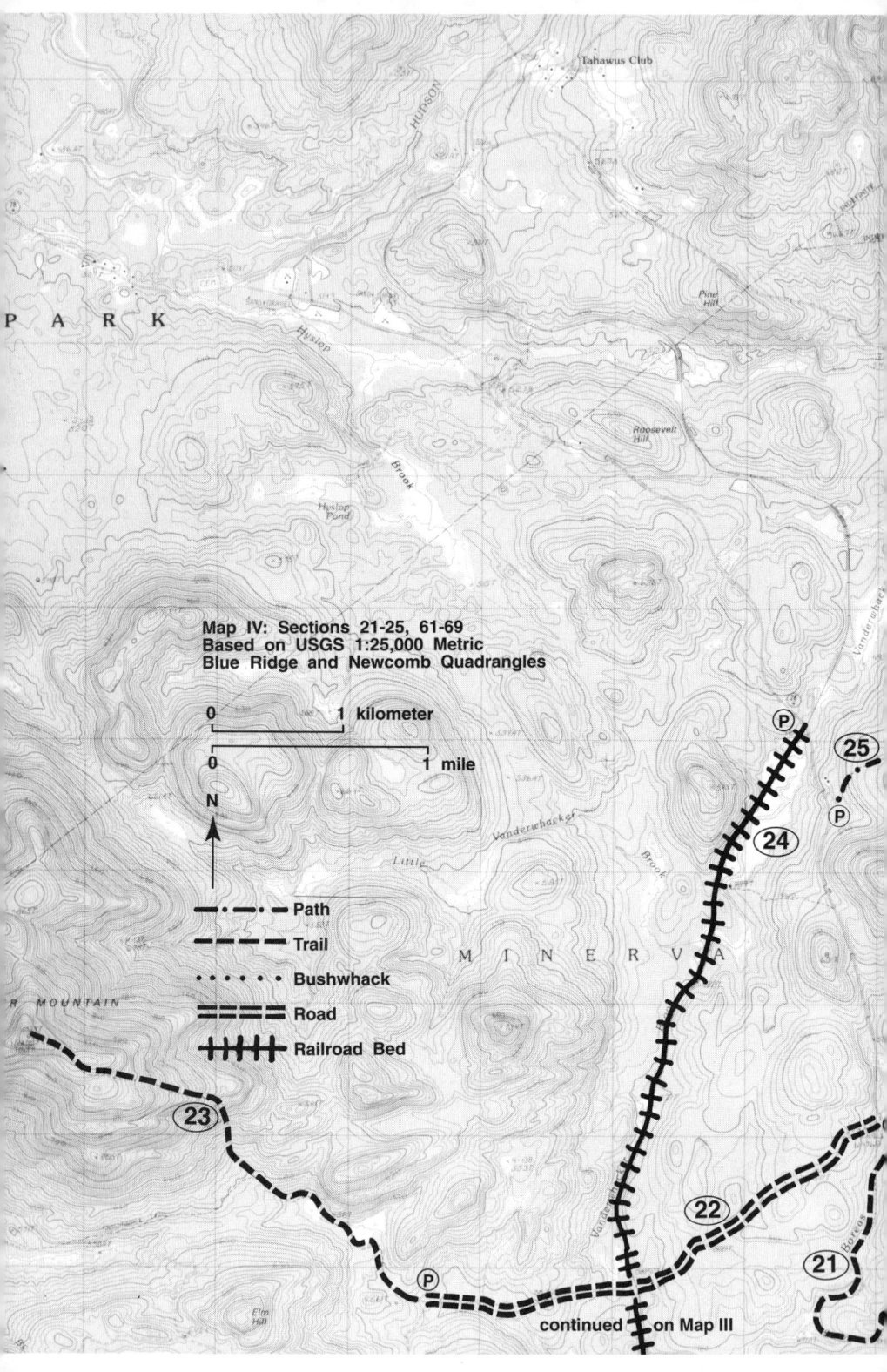

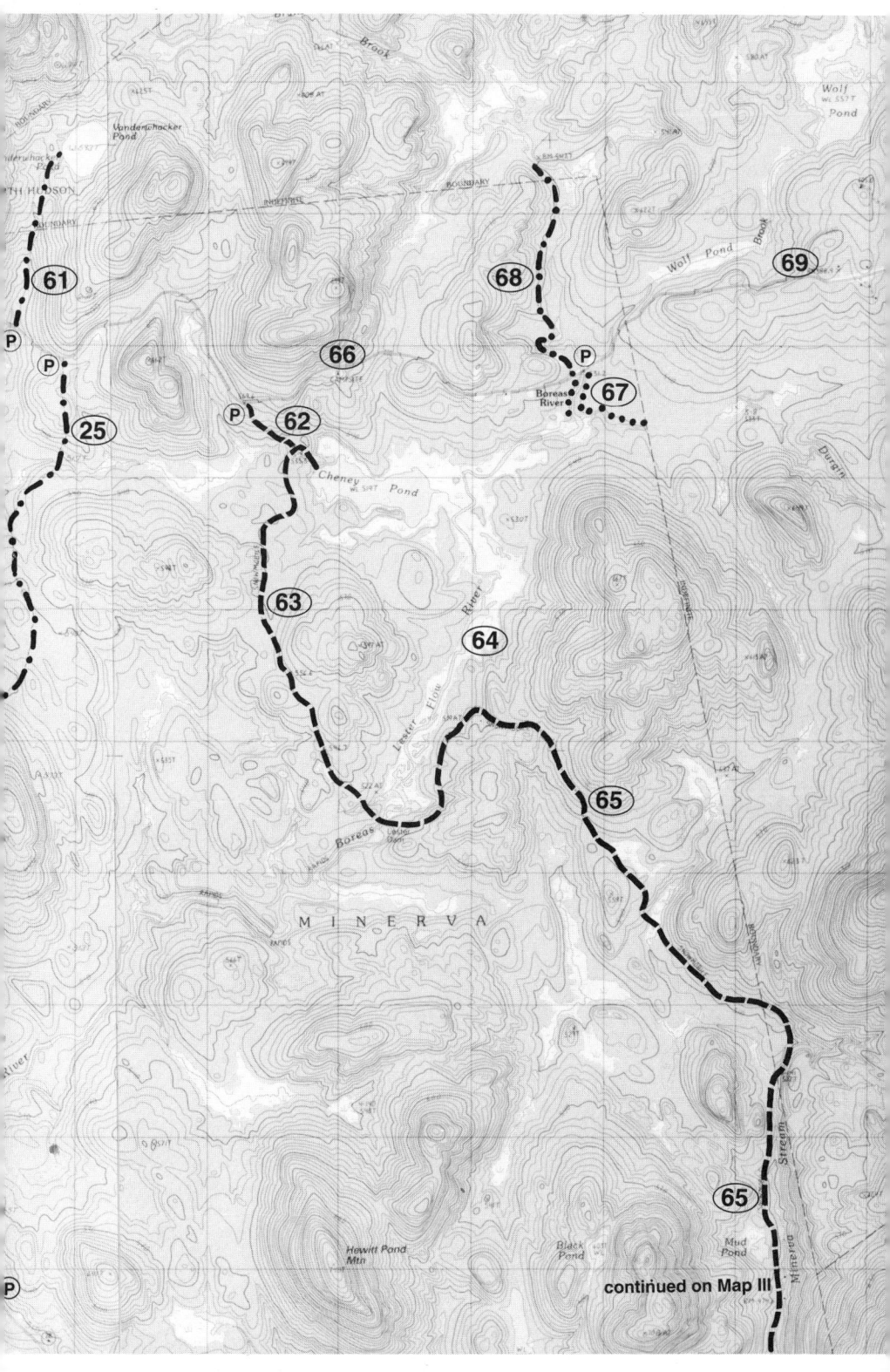

The northern half mile of trail is sheltered with tall spruce with views through the trunks to the stillwater which is never more than a few feet from the trail. The distances are short enough that you can make this loop with a single car, walking back on the road or retracing your steps on the trail.

22 Moose Pond Road
Camping, trailhead, maps III, IV

An unmarked dirt road heads west from NY 28 N, immediately north of the bridge over the Boreas. The roadsides are entirely on state land, up to a left fork, 2.6 miles in, which leads to the Moose Pond Club, a large private inholding which encompasses Moose, Bissell, and Fish ponds. Numerous camping turnouts border the first 1.5 miles of road which leads to a bridge over Vanderwhacker Brook and the D & H Railroad. Several very popular campsites border the road near the brook.

The trailhead for Vanderwhacker Mountain is 1.1 miles west of the brook at the point the Moose Pond Club Road forks left.

23 Vanderwhacker Mountain
Marked trail, fire tower, views, hiking, snowshoeing
5.8 miles round trip, 5 hours, 1700 feet (527 meters) vertical rise, red trail markers, maps III, IV

Isaac Vanderwhacker's name appears on the 1840 census for the Town of Minerva and his family included several well-known area loggers. Vanderwhacker is the most imposing mountain in the center of this region, a mammoth block rising in isolated splendor.

Vanderwhacker Mountain, elevation 3325 feet (1039 meters), was one of the mountains from which the surveyor Verplanck Colvin set signals to locate Adirondack peaks. He wrote:

> It commands a view of Mount Hamilton to the south-west and Prospect Hill to the southeast—two prominent primary signal stations.... The mountain was most easily approached from the village of Newcomb by a disused woods-road going southerly. From the terminus of this road on the west side of the mountain a trail goes easterly to the summit.

The modern trail is from the east and the Moose Pond Club Road. Since the fire tower has been manned in recent years, hikers have been able to enjoy a most spectacular view of the High Peaks to the north. From the tower you can trace the course of the Hudson south from Newcomb to the big bend near the confluence with the Indian. Snowy Mountain is visible in the distant southwest, Moxham Mountain to the south, and Hoffman Mountain and Texas Ridge to the east beyond the wide valley of the Boreas that was once Lester Flow.

The trail is in excellent shape, with chains of log stringers and bridges over small streams. The first 1.2 miles follow an old roadway beside the curved course of a small stream whose beaver marshes border the trail and whose flows occasionally dampen it. You meet the first of the new bridges after a ten-minute walk with a lovely pool beside the trail and pretty rock ledges. An enormous split-log bridge follows, then the trail circles south of a huge marsh. A second long marsh follows, over which you have your first close view of the shoulder of the mountain you are to climb. Another bridge over the stream follows; then the trail begins to rise.

At 1.5 miles, you see the two ranger's cabins in a small clearing—no camping is permitted here. The trail, with most (1300 feet) of the climbing and half the distance left, continues between the two cabins. The trail heads north, traversing a steep slope, then, after a fifteen-minute climb, levels out and swings west. Climbing more moderately, the trail crosses a draw and a small stream. From here to the summit, the trail alternates level stretches and pitches along a narrow ridge line, which gradually becomes enclosed in a sweet-smelling, walled corridor of spruce and balsam. The climb in this corridor along the knife-edge summit ridge takes over half an hour. The final stretch leading to the tower is fairly level. The climb from the cabins to the tower takes about an hour and a half.

Wait for a clear day for this one, for Vanderwhacker offers some of the best distant Adirondack views. Take cameras, and allow plenty of time on the summit.

24 Vanderwhacker Brook Stillwater
Short walk, reflections, canoeing, skiing, map IV

A dirt road leads west from NY 28 N, north of the Boreas bridge, to a very handsome private inholding at the foot of Vanderwhacker Brook Stillwater. State land starts a few hundred yards north of the road's end at the

Stillwater. It is possible to explore the state land portion of the Stillwater by walking south along the railroad tracks from the NY 28 N crossing or by carrying a canoe a short distance to put in on the brook itself. Distant views to the High Peaks reflect in the quiet water of the brook's many bends.

25 Old Roadway to the Blue Ridge Road
Cross-country skiing
2.7 miles, 1½ hours, 260 feet cumulative, map IV

2.3 miles north of the Boreas, or 0.3 mile south of the railroad crossing by Vanderwhacker Brook, there is a driveway on the east to a camp. The driveway ends in a picnic area with Forest Preserve markers from which a trail, following the old roadway, heads a little east of north to intersect the Blue Ridge Road 3.1 miles east of the railroad crossing near the road to Tahawus. The road was cleared as a snowmobile trail at one time, but the trail along it is not regularly maintained. Since the route goes nowhere, it would be best enjoyed as a cross-country ski trek. It is short enough to do the through trip twice from one parked vehicle. Note the steep pitch down from the hill on the north.

If you are looking to camp in the area, there is one other spot on the east side of the highway, 1.4 miles north of the Vanderwhacker Brook railroad crossing, 0.6 mile south of the Historical Marker which designates the road as the Roosevelt Memorial Highway. The turnout leads into a piney woods, no water, but secluded and close enough to the highway for an early start to some other destination.

North Woods Club Road

THE NORTH WOODS Club Road is a bumpy and, depending on the weather and season, muddy or dusty drive to the private North Woods Club, whose lands are posted. Though the end of the road is private, the best adventures in this guide are secreted along the route.

The road's history predates the fabled club by 31 years or more to 1854 when the Rev. Thomas Baker and his wife went into the woods to work for August Sherman, an early Adirondack lumberman. Baker was a preacher at the Wesleyan Methodist Church in Darrowsville, near Chestertown. Because of his opposition to slavery, he made his home a stop for slaves making their way on the underground railway to John Brown's home near North Elba.

For fifteen years the Bakers lived at the "Woods," acquiring and clearing land, farming, logging, and taking in lodgers and guests who hunted and fished. Their three-story log house developed a devoted clientele. Among the guests were John L. Fitch and Winslow Homer. Here Homer painted the log jam on the Hudson and scenes of fishing on the "Woods'" ponds. His vision of Mink Pond's dark, spruce-covered shores with Beaver Mountain behind became the symbol of a north-woods' pond.

The Bakers' daughter, Jennie, and her husband, Robert Bibby, bought out her family's interest in the property and ran a summer boarding house there after 1878. So popular was the place with former guests that they formed the Adirondack Preserve Association to buy the property in 1886. With the addition of more land the next year, the group, with the new name, North Woods Club, held 5000 acres. Members included Andrew Mellon, Henry Clay Frick, Alfred R. Whitney, and Winslow Homer, who drew inspiration from the club's woods and ponds for many summers. His paintings of trout fishing and Mink Pond are the visual image most of us have of the north woods.

Bibby stayed on as caretaker, building a sawmill whose lumber he used to build a new barn, farm house, and many new cottages. The latter were of a distinctive, rustic character, large and dark, with covered porches—good

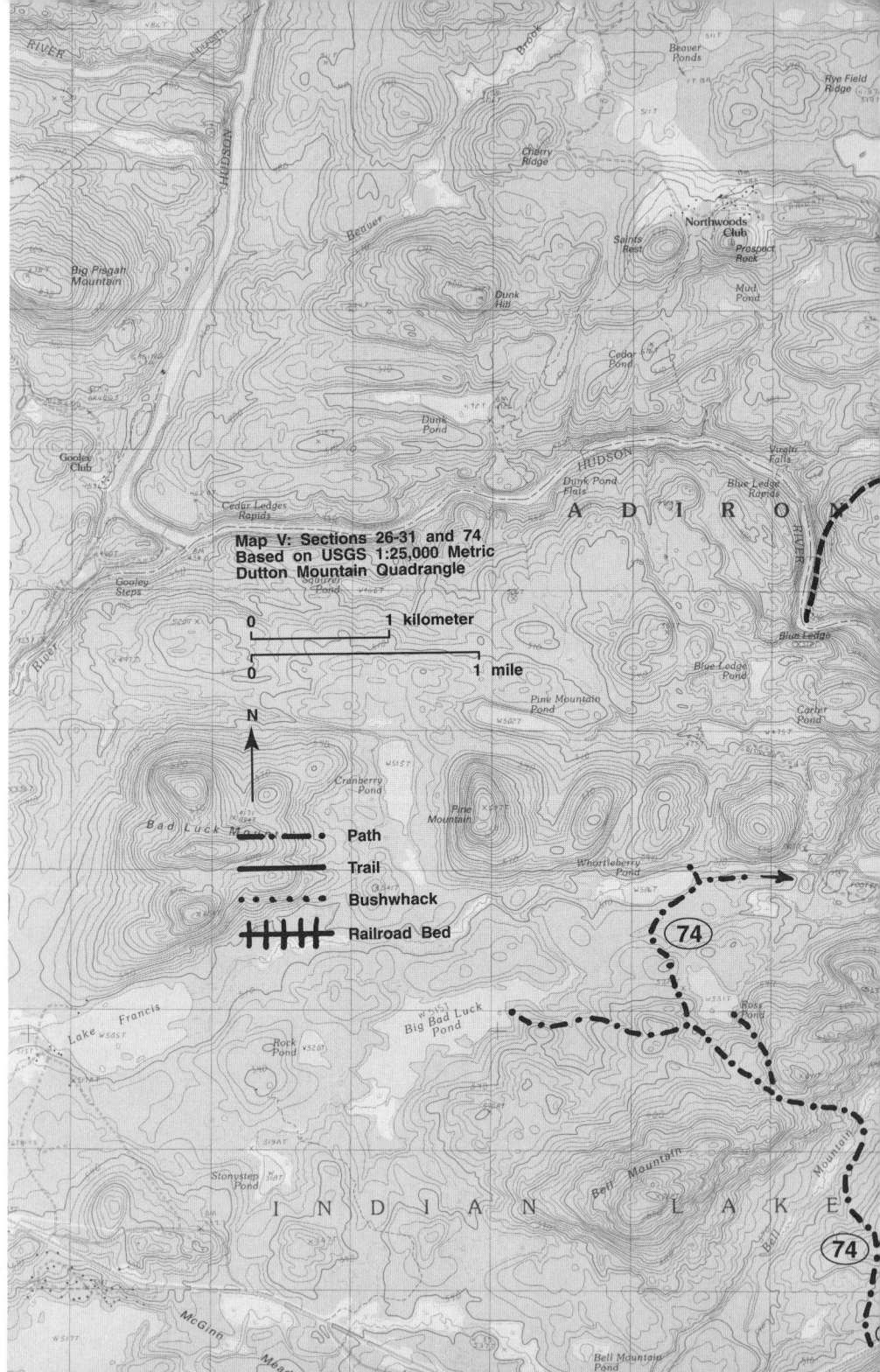

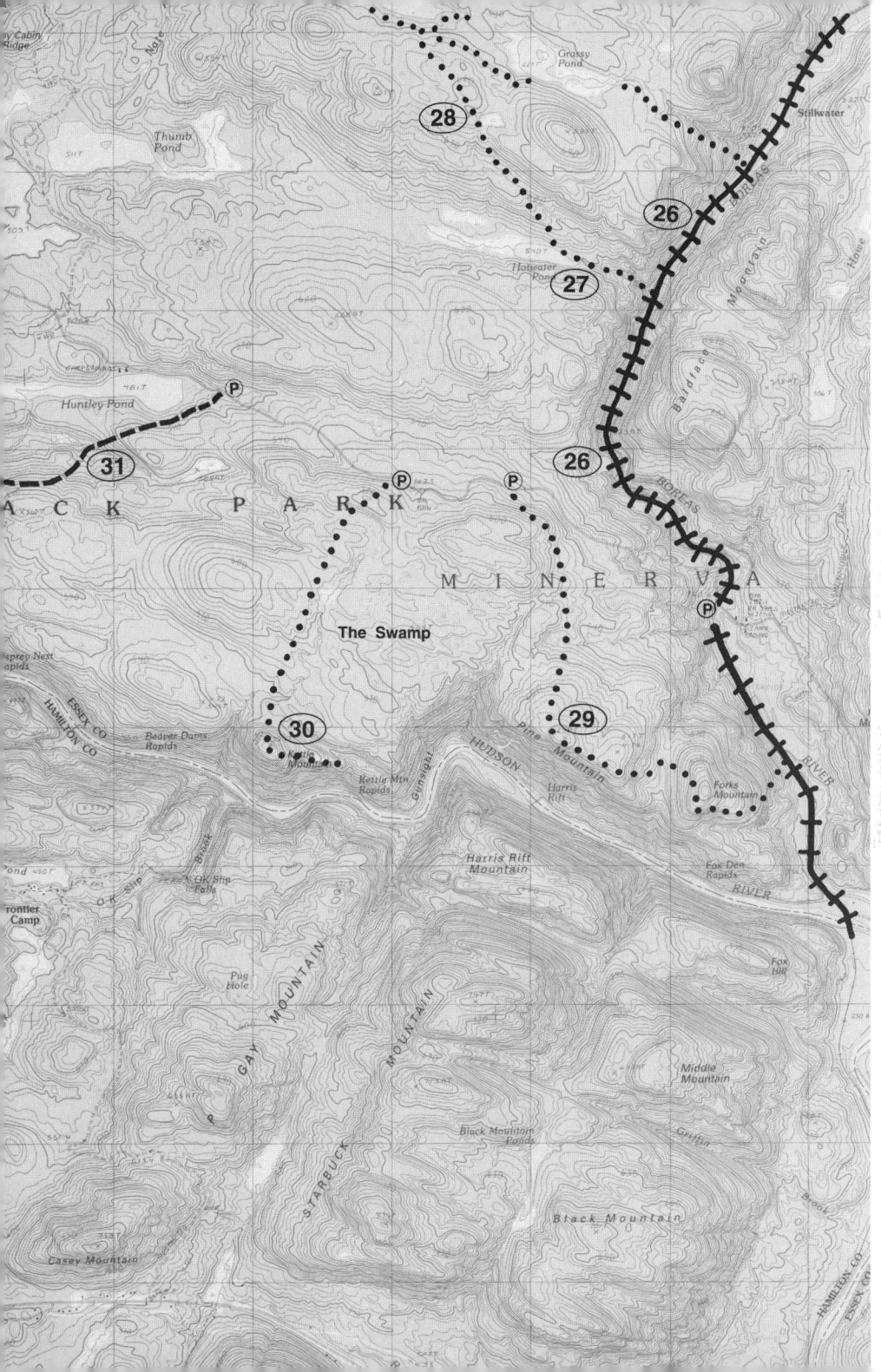

examples of the Adirondack "camp." The club survives today. Its lands at the end of the North Woods Club Road are posted and off limits to the public.

26 The Railroad from the North Woods Club Road to the Moose Pond Road
Walking, exploring
5.5 miles, 2¼ hours, flat, maps III, V

Walking along the right-of-way of a railroad may not sound like a wilderness trek, but you should become acquainted with this route for the adventures to which it will lead you. The railroad is a relative newcomer to the Adirondacks, built in 1942 under the wartime emergency, which took precedence over the sanctity of the Forest Preserve. It was built to extend the North Creek Line of the D & H to the mine at Tahawus with its valuable titanium deposits. This stretch follows the Boreas River and allows you to become acquainted with a handsome part of the river, and it is a remarkably pleasant walk.

With a car spotted at each end, a through walk can be accomplished in just over two hours. Consult section 22 for a description of parking at the northern end. The tracks are not currently being used.

Drive the North Woods Club Road 3.8 miles west from NY 28 N to the bridge over the Boreas. The last mile is a long traverse on the shoulder of Kellogg Mountain, a delightful drive through a mature hemlock forest. At the last crest before the river, there is a parking turnout on the right. A short dirt road leads left down the east shore of the river to several campsites. If you go straight ahead, across the bridge, you will find another campsite on the right, upstream. The road crosses the railroad tracks 200 yards from the bridge. Park nearby.

The railroad makes a series of deep curves as it follows the river's course north, and in 0.5 mile you will want to leave the tracks to observe the gorge far below the tracks. Watch as the tracks pass through a blasted cut in the mountainside for it exposes a brilliant outcrop of blue calcite.

North of the last big curve, just over a mile, the track straightens out. All along this straight stretch, the river is your constant companion, not always visible from the tracks, but with many beautiful rapids always audible.

Railroad beside Boreas Stillwater

The stream emerging from mountainside at 1.8 miles, a forty-minute walk, is the outlet of Hot Water Pond (section 27). Ten minutes more, 0.7 mile, brings you to the beginning of a double track and a railroad sign marking the Stillwater Siding; 150 feet south of the sign walk down to streamside to discover a hunter's cable used to cross the Boreas in high water.

Near the north end of the double-track siding the railroad overlooks a quiet stretch of river known as Stillwater. This was the site of Sheldon (Bob) Hewitt's camp, the hunter who guided the naturalist John Burroughs on his Adirondack birding trip (see sections 27 and 28). Here, on a trek along the Boreas, he caught six trout in less than twenty minutes, "three of them over one foot long each," besting his guide and earning his respect.

Spruce swamps border the river here, and the outlet of Fish Pond flows into a marsh to the west of the tracks 0.5 mile north of Stillwater Junction.

In the next 1.5 miles, the river is only occasionally visible from the tracks. After the outlet of Moose Pond flows in from the west, the rail bed is in a large marshy area with a good view of the big bend in the Boreas. Here the tracks turn away from the river which bends west. A five-minute walk along the tracks takes you to the Moose Pond Road.

27 The Burroughs Caves and Hot Water Pond
Bushwhack, cave exploration, map V

John Burroughs is well known for the writing inspired by the surroundings of his Catskill home. In 1863, when Burroughs was 26, he traveled to the Adirondacks to pursue his newly begun study of birds. So impressed was he by what he saw that the trip appears to be a turning point in his career, for this marks the beginning of his writing career which spanned twenty volumes and nearly fifty years.

Later, he wrote in *Wake Robin* about his Adirondack adventures:

When I went to the Adirondacks, which was in the summer of 1863, I was in the first flush of my ornithological studies, and was curious above all else to know what birds I should find in these solitudes,—what new ones and what ones already known to me. In visiting vast, primitive far-off woods, one naturally expects to find something rare and precious and something entirely new. But it commonly happens that one is disappointed. This was about my own experience in the Adirondacks. The birds prefer the vicinity of settlements and clearings and it was at such a place that I saw the greatest number and variety . . . purple finches, pine finches (grosbeaks), and Canada, black-throated blue, yellow-rumped, and Audubon's warblers . . . Birds of any kind were rare in these woods. A pigeon hawk came by prowling our camp, and the faint piping call of the nuthatches, leading their young through the high trees, was often heard.

The caves, however, did not disappoint him:

One afternoon we visited a cave some two miles down the stream [the Boreas]. We squeezed and wriggled through a big cleft in the side of the mountain for about two hundred feet, when we emerged into a large dome-shaped passage, the abode, during certain seasons of innumerable bats and at all times of primeval darkness. The voice of running water was heard everywhere, betraying the proximity of the little stream by whose ceaseless corroding the cave and its entrance had been worn. This streamlet flowed out of the mouth of the cave and came from a lake at the top of the mountain. This accounted for its warmth to the hand which surprised us all.

The caves have been eroded by the outlet of Hot Water Pond, named not because its water is warmer than other Adirondack ponds but because its emergence from the ground at the cave entrance is not the cool spring you would expect.

The forty-minute, 1.8-mile walk beside the railroad tracks should take you near the north end of the long straight stretch of track. You have to look for the small stream which emerges from the hillside: then it is easy to spot a small path north of the stream which climbs the bank and plunges immediately into a deep glen. The path follows the stream with its moss-covered rocks. Ledges flank the south side of the stream.

You climb steeply and within ten minutes, you reach a small cirque from which two small streams flow. Go straight up the headwall to the left, scrambling up past a small waterfall, picking your way to the cave entrance from which the stream emerges. Long lacy fronds of *Cystopteris bulbifera*, the berry bulblet fern, drape the opening. A very few specimens of a rare gem, the slender cliffbrake fern, *Cryptogramma stelleri*, are also found on the wall. Hiding in deep moist shade, this fern lives only in soils rich in limestone. They are a clue to the rocks from which the caves have been formed, a Grenville series, metamorphosed sedimentary rock known as skarn, composed of metamorphosed sand, clay, and limestone. The largest portion of the limestone has become marble, chips of which remain to cut your hands if you make your way into the cave.

Depending on the water level, you can squeeze past the stream and climb upward through several passages to the small room. (Hardhats and flashlights are a must, but no ropes are necessary.) On the way you pass folds outlined in the silicate-rich hornfels where the surrounding marbles have been weathered away by flowing water. These appear on the cave wall as Corinthian capitols. Grains of calcite glitter underfoot. In the room, a solution cave—created where the water dissolved the marble, perhaps twenty feet in diameter and twice that high—you can hear the stream rushing through a passage far below. Piled boulders let you climb part way up through the room.

Two other smaller openings in the cirque beckon the practiced spelunker.

The adventure does not end with exploring the caves; continue climbing out of the cirque, angling north to climb to the plateau on top. Pick a course toward the west keeping a deep ravine to your right. The open woods are delightful with Goldies fern, long beech fern, *Gymnocarpium* or oak fern, and maidenhair. Within a ten-minute walk from the cave, less than 0.5 mile from the railroad, you can spot Hot Water Pond through the trees. Before you reach it though, you will discover three large sink holes, all less than 100 yards from the pond. Their walls are moist with ferns and mosses. One is more than 20 feet deep with the outlet disappearing through a hole in the bottom.

Careful scrambling should permit you to descend them all and explore the place where the stream disappears to continue eroding the caves beneath. What other chambers lie between here and the cirque?

The pond is very shallow with boggy shores and a large marsh in the middle. Beaver have capped the natural rock outlet with a dam. Hikers have camped near the outlet. After flowing over the beaver dam, the outlet disappears into one of the sink holes.

28 Nates and Grassy Ponds
Bushwhack, camping, fishing, map V

A long day's bushwhack will let you follow Burroughs' steps to Nates Pond, then back to the railroad via Grassy Pond and its outlet. Burroughs continued from Nates Pond northwest to Tahawus. He described the first portion of this trip in *Wake Robin:*

> Pressing on through the forest we reached our destination, Nate's Pond—a pretty sheet of water, lying like a silver mirror in the lap of the mountain, a very picture of unbroken solitude. It is not possible for the woods alone to give one an impression of utter lonlyness [sic]. In the woods are sounds and voices, and a dumb kind of companionship, one is little more than a walking tree himself; but come upon one of these mountain lakes and the wilderness stands revealed and meets you face to face. Water is thus facile and adaptive, that makes it the wild more wild, while it enhances culture and art. Those who lodge with Nature find early rising quite in order. The camper-out feels morning in the air, he smells it, sees it, hears it, and springs up with the

Boreas River

general awakening. Nate's Pond contains perch and sunfish but no trout . . . By the lake I met that orchard beauty, the cedar waxwing, spending his vacation in the assumed character of a fly catcher, whose part he performed with great accuracy and deliberation . . . Here, also, I met my beautiful singer, the hermit thrush, but with no song in his throat now. This was the only species of thrush I saw in the Adirondacks.

From the eastern end of Hot Water Pond, pick a course of 340° magnetic. You will be climbing 300 feet in a long, gentle traverse of about a mile to level ground and the short, 0.5 mile, descent to the pond. The understory is not too thick, but it will take an hour and a half for the traverse.

When you reach the south shore of Nate's Pond, you will find Beaver Mountain beautifully situated to the northwest of this crystal sheet. If you are lucky enough to find the secreted boat, you can explore all of the pond's 0.4-mile length. (Remember the sportsman's code: you can borrow his boat if you return it exactly as you found it to its hiding place.)

From the northwest shore of the pond, a path heads due north through a notch to Fish Pond, following old trails and new logging roads. However, this route quickly leads to the private lands of the Moose Pond Club. There is a campsite where the path heads away from Nates pond.

The 0.5 mile or so between Nates Pond and Grassy Pond to the east is a swampy divide between two watersheds, wet and formidable, a "spruce bog" with all the horrible images that phrase conjurs: spongy sphagnum underfoot; sharp, tangled, and brittle dead branches impeding your way; fallen trees with branches thrust up to trip your every step; and the dark, dense shade of spruce making it impossible to see where you are headed. That should convince you to head for higher ground and bushwack east paralleling the swamp. The steeper south side of the divide is best. The western shore of Grassy Pond is so dense I was within 10 feet of its bordering marsh before it became visible!

Old maps show Grassy Pond was originally named Bloody Moose Pond, and you can imagine a moose standing along its shores, silhouetted against the bordering dark spruce and hemlock. The entire shore is a sphagnum mat, sometimes crowned with clumps of grass or more often with dense shrubs like leatherleaf. Two or three boulders offer dry perches for resting as you push your way east toward the outlet. There is a tiny rocky island in the center of the pond.

From the beaver dam at the outlet, take a course of magnetic east, and you will quickly leave the spruce thickets. This course intersects the outlet again, where it begins to descend steeply. Stay south of the outlet to complete the 0.8 mile, 540-foot descent from the outlet, a bushwhack of at least three-quarters of an hour.

You reach the tracks about 200 yards north of the beginning of the double track near Stillwater. It takes 20 minutes to walk back to the outlet of Hot Water Pond, an hour to return to the Moose Woods Club Road. Most of the bushwhack segments outlined are fairly strenuous. If you enrich this loop with a visit to the caves, a sojourn at Nates Pond, and time to savor this heart of the north woods, the loop outlined becomes a ten-hour day.

29 Pine and Forks Mountains
Bushwhack, maps V

From west of Blue Ledge to its confluence with the Boreas, the Hudson River plunges a little south of east through a deep gorge with mountains rising precipitously from the broad, turbulent rapids of the rock-strewn riverbed. Here in less than 6 miles, the river drops over 300 feet. The enclosing walls of the gorge rise as high as 900 feet to a high plateau on the north that is carved into a chain of mountains. These mountains have steep faces and cliffs on their south faces and gentle hillsides descending to the plateau on the north. Pine Mountain is the tallest north of the Hudson. Kettle, Pine, and Forks mountains all have excellent views; and all can be easily reached by bushwhacks.

The Hudson River Gorge was formed as the result of a long period of continuous erosion by the ancestral Hudson River. The erosion continues to this day while the adjacent mountain region is uplifted, and the river naturally erodes a course through rocks that are most easily abraded, dissolved, and worn away.

The Hudson flows generally westward from Tahawus to Harris Lake in a zone of weak Grenville marbles. At Harris Lake it turns south and flows partly in a U-shaped synclinal fold in the granitic syenite rocks. The fold was formed by flow lines that developed in the rocks as they solidified slowly from molten magma at great depth millions of years earlier.

At the Gooley Club, the confluence of the Indian, the Hudson turns generally east as it again erodes its way through a belt of weak Grenville marbles. The marbles are well exposed at Blue Ledge at the foot of the trail from Huntley Pond (section 31). The easily eroded Grenville marbles at river level are overlain by the syenite sills which produce the steep walls of this remarkably beautiful canyon.

East of Kettle Mountain, the river has cut through a section of the syenite. This crosscut is reflected by the northward jog in the river's course, just up river from Harris Rift rapids and about one-and-a-half miles east of Kettle Mountain. After rushing through the syenite jog, the river reenters the more easily eroded Grenville marbles and continues eastward. At the river junction where the Boreas enters from the north, the Hudson encounters the resistant syenite sills of Dutton Mountain. The belt of Grenville marbles sharply bends to the south here, and the Hudson follows this path of least resistance. The river changes course to the south, crosses the ledge of Greyhound Bus rapids, and continues bending east again at the hamlet of North River.

To begin to explore the geology as well as the scenery of the gorge, you can make a fairly easy bushwhack circuit of Pine and Forks Mountains. The circuit can be extended to a visit to the confluence of the Boreas as well. Your group may want to spot a car where the North Woods Club Road crosses the Boreas and drive a second car uphill 1.4 miles to 1700-foot elevation where there is a turnout for one or two cars. Head east of

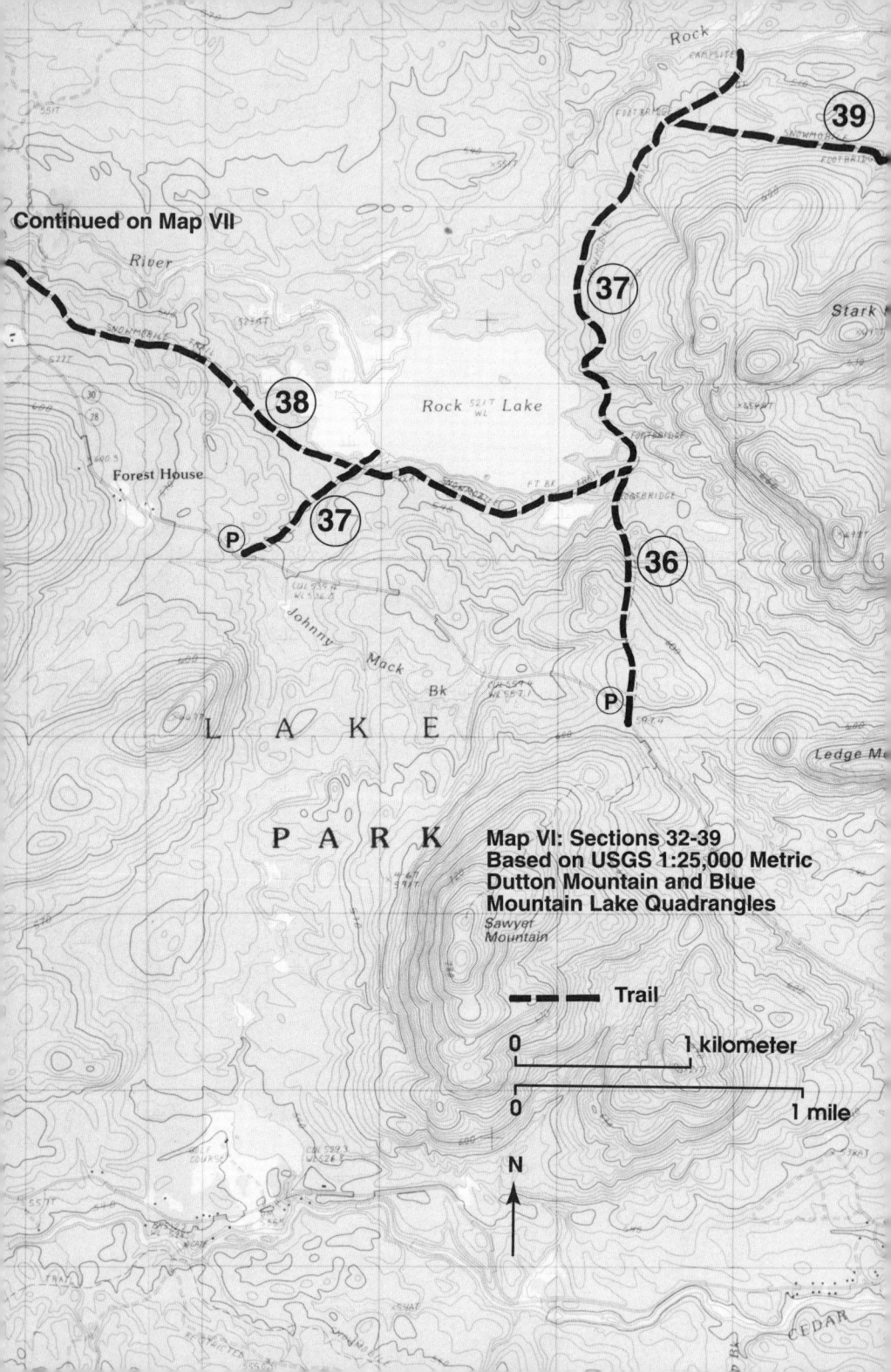

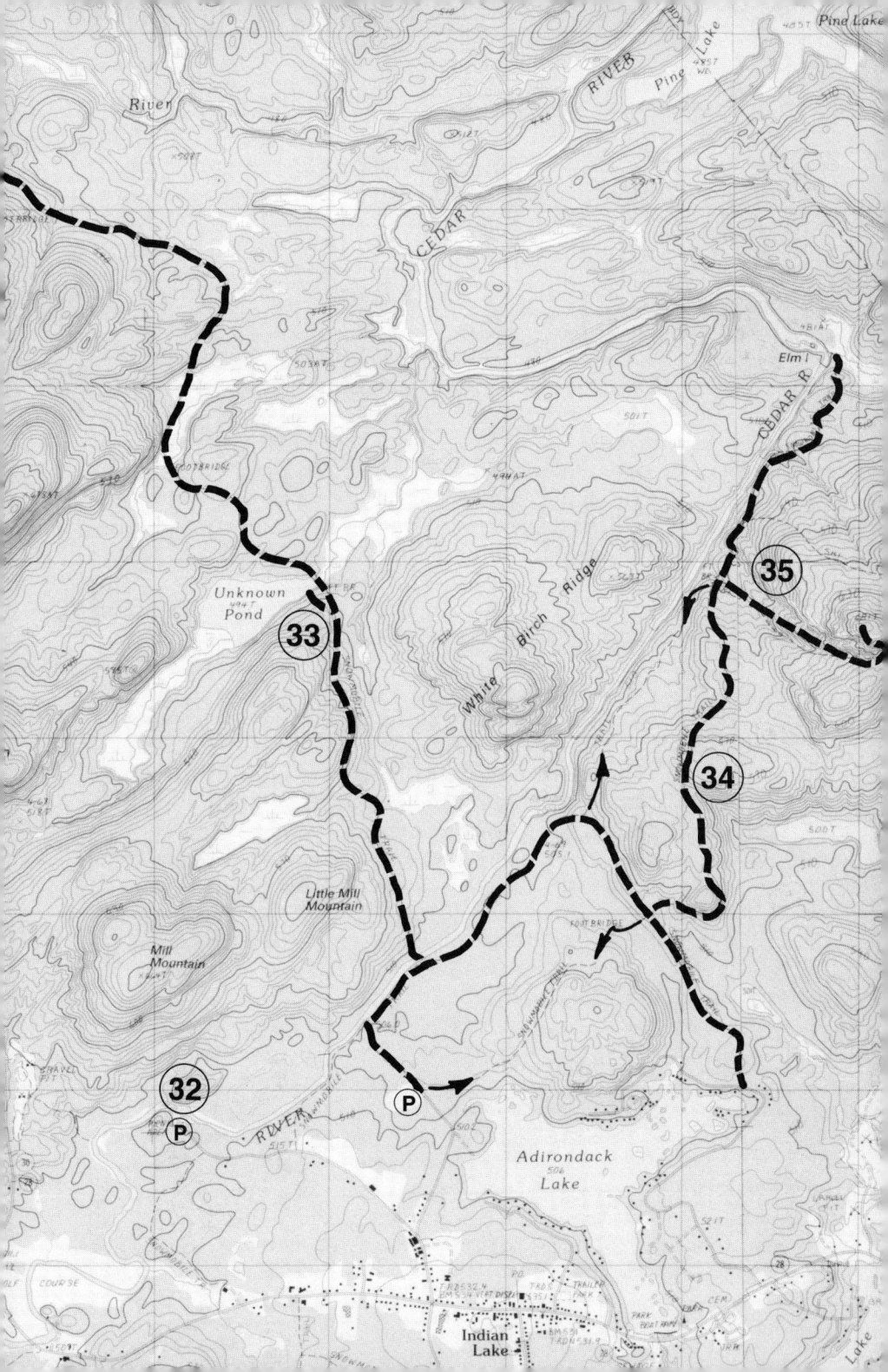

south into the woods, contouring just above the 1700-foot level around a small hillside. An altimeter is helpful here to keep you on course. The route takes you across two small streams.

Keeping elevation forces you to change course to a more southerly direction and in 0.8 mile you cross a third stream. Continue south, beginning a gentle climb through open woods, climbing layers of pink and gray granitic syenite that dip mostly north away from the Hudson Gorge. The southerly course over these sills will bring you to the open edge of Pine Mountain above Harris Rift within an hour. The 1.5-mile bushwhack is that easy!

From everywhere along this open edge, there are glimpses seemingly straight down to the rift and across to Harris Rift Mountain with Starbuck behind. Blueberries abound on the south-facing summit line. Walk west until you can see Kettle Mountain and the big curve in the Hudson. The roar of the rapids belies the fact the river is 900 feet below.

Then follow the ridge line back east, continuing until you start to descend. Angle a bit north to cross at the high point of the saddle between Pine and Forks mountains. The ridge line is so open that the walk from the western view point to the saddle, 0.9 mile, takes less than half an hour.

The gentle climb to Forks Mountain's triangular summit is easy at first though pockets of spruce cover the top. To cross the summit you cannot avoid them all. There are no good views from the southern apex, but you will find some through-the-trees views along the eastern edges of the summit. Walk northeast, descending only slightly, and you will reach a large, open patch after a half-hour trek from the saddle.

This is obviously the same fire-scarred patch from which Robert Balk drew a sketch of the confluence of the Hudson and the Boreas with Dutton Mountain in the background (see the 1932 Geology of the Newcomb Triangle, New York State Museum). Recovery from fire has been slow because of the steepness of the mountain and the thin soil that remained after the fire.

The view is superb, and it is a great place for a picnic. To descend, head generally north, losing elevation where you can. It is a steep mountainside! Your traverse should take you down 650 feet in short order to a point on the railroad tracks half-way between the North Woods Club Road and the rivers' confluence. Turn south along the tracks for twenty minutes until you see the bridge over the Hudson. Immediately north of it, there is a path headed east to the long, thin, forested spit of land and sand bars that formed when the rivers were much more substantial in their glacial past. Beneath the huge white pines, there is a lovely camping spot. This is the place you viewed from the fire-scarred area on Forks Mountain.

A forty-minute walk will take you from the confluence, back to the tracks and north to the North Woods Club Road, a distance of 2 miles. Allow at least six hours for the entire circuit.

30 Kettle Mountain
Bushwhack, map V

Until the state acquires OK Slip Falls, whose height, about 250 feet, makes it one of the Adirondacks' most spectacular, the public has no access to it. However, you can enjoy an unusual view of it from the south-facing ledges of Kettle Mountain, less than 0.4 mile away.

Drive 1.8 miles west of the Boreas Bridge on the North Woods Club Road. There is a parking turnout near the height-of-land. You will start the bushwhack about 0.2 mile on down the road.

A 1.5-mile bushwhack, west of south, 200° magnetic, will take you to open ledges on Kettle's summit in an hour and a half. Several small ridges lie along the outlined route. You climb one knoll, skirt west around a wet area, climb a second knoll, and continue west of a small valley. After 0.7 mile, you descend slightly; change course to due south, crossing the stream in the valley and begin climbing toward Kettle's summit. The climb up Kettle at the end is quite gentle.

Depending where you reach the summit, you can range along the cliff tops to the best vantages from which to view OK Slip Falls. Look for other openings on the west side of the summit; one faces directly west upriver with Snowy Mountain on the horizon. Another opening on the north side of the mountain allows a view of Vanderwhacker Mountain. Fires have ravaged this mountainside. Lichens are pioneering on the rock ledges. It is a fragile place so try to walk on the open rock.

There is, however, an interesting pitfall which you could encounter. Just to the east of the course, to the east of the valley and stream but northeast of Kettle's summit, lies an enormous cedar swamp. This large diamond-shaped area, three quarters of a mile by over half a mile, begins less than 0.5 mile from the road. The swamp formed where surface water was prevented from draining away by the underlying flat bedrock sill. This is the sort of place that added "dismal and abysmal swamp" to so many early descriptions of the great north woods. Cedar was so valuable that much of this Adirondack resource was harvested in the nineteenth century, and few areas have recovered to their original extent.

A cedar swamp is a wild place. Cedar is so slow to decay that the swamp is typically multilayered with fallen logs. The trees grow from deep sphagnum mats and pools of standing water. This swamp has several small watercourses and a number of small beaver flows. Even if you do not inadvertently stray off course into it, you may want to visit this historical relic.

31 Blue Ledge and Huntley Pond
Marked trail, swimming, picnicking
2.3 miles one way, 1½ hours, 300 feet elevation change, blue markers, map V

The only marked route to the Hudson's fabled northern ledges descends from the North Woods Club Road directly to the river without the cliff top views the bushwhacks offer. The trail ends beneath the Blue Ledge, which rises abruptly for 300 feet across the river on the south. In summer, quiet swimming pools fill niches in the river's course which, in the spring, are frenzied whirlpools. The ledges cool the site year-round, and there is a crevice in them in which ravens nest each year in spring.

The trail begins on the south side of the North Woods Club Road, 3 miles from the Boreas Bridge, and just east of Huntley Pond. The road parallels Huntley Pond briefly, and there are several traditional campsites near the pond close to the road. Some of these may be closed because they have been abused but if you want to camp, it is relatively easy to find other sites.

The blue-marked footpath heads up away from the pond, generally west-southwest. It crosses a stream at 0.5 mile, climbs gently around a hillside, and at 1.2 miles intersects an old logging road. The trail follows the roadway toward the Hudson, staying south of a beaver meadow.

The path makes a definite turn to the south at 1.5 miles and climbs a knoll where already you can begin to hear the river. The trail, now only a narrow footpath, parallels the river in its southward bend and gradually descends to water level at 2.3 miles. Tall pines shelter the trail as it makes its way down to the river. Short paths lead both up and downstream along the river where the shore is so steep there is barely room for a picnic. Campers have, however, managed to find a few level places.

Three hours suffice for a walk to the river and back, but the beauty of the spot deserves a full day's outing.

Indian Lake to Blue Mountain Lake to Long Lake

NO INTRODUCTION THAT this guide could give to the Blue Mountain Lake area would be so vivid or comprehensive as the pictures and exhibits you can see on a visit to the Adirondack Museum, which is open from the end of May until early October. The history of the region's lake resorts is much better documented than the history of the relatively little known interior areas.

In 1847 Father Olivetti bought Township 17, which includes Rock Lake as well as what is now Indian Lake Village. In 1851 he added 12,500 acres to his holdings, the southern half of Township 19, which included the land between Blue Mountain and Tirrell Pond but bordering the pond only at its southern end. He induced a group of Irish immigrants to move to the tract and clear the wilderness. The pond is named for his foreman, Pat Tirrell. This settlement was short-lived, perhaps no more than two years.

Chauncey Hawthorn built a guest house at Tirrell Pond in 1870, and another place to accommodate hunters and fishermen was later built, only to be burned by the state as it acquired the land for the Forest Preserve. Visitors to Blue Mountain Lake might spend a night or so at Tirrell Pond, fishing and enjoying its wilderness atmosphere.

A settlement grew up around logging operations and sawmills on the Cedar River, but these, too, have disappeared.

32 Cedar River and Pasley Falls
Canoeing, picnicking, access to hiking, map VI

Turn north, right, on Belong Road, which is 0.5 mile west of the intersection of NY 30 and 28 in Indian Lake Village. Turn left at the first fork and go to the end of the road—a delightful picnic spot and boat launch on the Cedar River. Depending on the height of the water, there may be a fairly strong current; but it is all flat water north on the Cedar to Pasley Falls. Make this delightful canoe trip for 2 miles downstream, pulling out on the west bank before the falls to climb the cliffs above the falls for a picnic.

Watch as you canoe north after paddling for 1.2 miles, about half an hour. You should spot snowmobile trail signs on the west bank. You can pull your canoe on shore here and walk to Unknown Pond, a trip that without a canoe can only be made in winter.

33 Unknown Pond
Hiking, cross-country skiing, snowmobile trail
1.5 miles, relatively level, map VI

Head for Unknown Pond as part of a winter ski trip (section 34) after skiing 0.8 mile from the trailhead; or hike from the shore of the Cedar River after paddling downstream 1.2 miles from the launch site to the trailhead.

This is a relatively level walk on a fine trail through a majestic forest of tall, straight yellow birch and cherry. Snowmobile bridges make it especially easy walking as does the fact the pond is only twenty feet below the trailhead at the river crossing. You contour around two small hills. In winter you can look back early on in the trip and see the rocky south face of McGinn Mountain in the distance through the trees.

In just over a thirty-minute walk, you see an opening through the trees on your left. The trail has begun a steep descent; 100 feet down there is a fork. The snowmobile trail stays right. It leads into the huge marsh below Unknown Pond. Go left on a path that leads to the outlet of the 38-acre pond. From rocks at the outlet of the pond you can look across to Ledge Mountain and an unnamed hill, both of which exhibit the signature-curving cliffs and slides that distinguish the Blue Mountain area. Be careful, though, for the outlet rocks are laced with poison ivy. Across the dam a path climbs to the ridge above the marsh where there is a nice camping spot and continues on to rejoin the snowmobile trail. If you take a short hike west along the south shore, you can see the slopes and rock slides of the Stark Hills with Blue Mountain in the background.

34 Pasley Falls and Elm Island
Snowmobile trail, hiking, fishing, cross-country skiing
4.7 miles one way, 2½ hours, relatively level, map VI

A marked snowmobile trail with three beginnings leads to Elm Island, a bend in the Cedar River about halfway between Indian Lake Village and the Hudson River. The three trails suggest a number of loops for skiers who want a bit of exercise close to the village though skiers are cautioned to watch out for snowmobiles. The three beginnings fulfill the promise of Greenline Parks, for a resident can walk or ski from the village to a wilderness route.

A fourth segment, north of Pasley Falls, which was marked as a ski trail, parallels the snowmobile trail, but closer to the Cedar River. It is too overgrown and has so many missing markers that it no longer serves as a hiking route and is definitely too full of blowdowns to serve as a ski route. It is not described in this section though the places where it intersects the rest of the network are described.

Turn right on Belong Road and stay right when it forks; this route leads to the town landfill. Park just before the landfill gate. A roadway continues straight ahead; a second roadway turns right. Either will take you to Elm Island. Consult the map for the connectors; only the route closest to the river is described in detail. The third beginning is from Adirondack Lake Road, which is just east of the village. Drive northwest on it for 1.4 miles to the beginning of the connector, which is an 0.8-mile link to the network. It joins the network at a four-way intersection described below.

Heading straight ahead, northwest, beside the dump site (marked Unknown Pond), you reach the river at 0.4 mile and turn right along it. (A fifth spur trail leads snowmobilers left along the river and back to the golf course.)

Both snowmobile and ski trail signs mark the route, which briefly splits, with the ski trail staying closest to the river. A 0.3-mile walk along the river puts the rejoined routes opposite the trail to Unknown Pond; here is where skiers and snowmobilers can cross when the river is frozen solid.

The narrow trail now winds northeast beside the river but farther and farther from it. Forty minutes from the start, at 1.6 miles, you hear the rapids at Pasley Falls long before you see them. The trail climbs a knoll behind the bend in the river and you have to leave it to see the falls, which are a series of rapids pinched between cliffs that wall in the river here.

Just past the closest approach to the falls, the trail begins to climb again, now to the west. A yellow-marked ski trail forks right here and heads back to the alternate snowmobile trail; it is a marked shortcut to Lake Adirondack. A marked ski trail—the one that has all but disappeared—forks left here. You stay straight, uphill and back southwest. The trail passes a marvelous cedar swamp and an enormous white pine with a label stating it is "118" around"; and 0.6 mile from the falls, at 2.2 miles, the trail reaches a four-way intersection. The way right leads back 1.2 miles to the trailhead by the dump; the way straight ahead leads 0.8 mile to Lake Adirondack Road. Obviously if you are just heading to Elm Island and do not care about the falls, either of these beginnings are shorter but certainly less attractive.

The way left is the old road to Elm Island, and a sign marking it says to McGinn Mountain Trail. This marked snowmobile trail heads briefly west

Views of Elm Island

and uphill, then north along a hillside that slopes off to the right. The trail winds up and down, taking a relatively dull course for forty minutes when it begins a steep descent. In the midst of this descent, 1.5 miles from the four-way intersection, there is a very strange pair of intersections: the other end of the overgrown ski trail comes in on the left, crosses the trail, rejoins it, and finally heads right for McGinn Mountain near the point the snowmobile trail crosses a small stream on a bridge.

The snowmobile route is still above the level of the river, though you occasionally glimpse it through the trees. You walk for another mile, about thirty minutes, before heading sharply down, zigzagging, then turning right along the river for 150 yards to emerge in a grassy field beside the bend above Elm Island. This lovely spot is bordered on the west by small cliffs; lesser purple-fringed orchis bloom at streamside. Here, where snowmobiles turn around in winter and where a small brook comes in from Corner Pond to the east, you find an excellent camping spot.

The gorge, upriver, is steep, rocky, and impressive. In winter an ice jam usually occurs above the bend; huge ice cakes tumble together in a haphazard, jagged morass. Some winters the ice reaches almost to the top of the cliffs. If you try to ski out on it, watch for deep holes beside some of the blocks which are deceptively covered with snow.

Pasley Falls

As the river turns west toward low-lying Elm Island, it calms and offers a chance for a pleasant dip after a warm summer hike. It is a pristine spot; and, except for logging years ago, it is true wilderness, for there has never been a settlement or any farming along this stretch of river.

35 McGinn Mountain
Bushwhack, hiking, snowshoeing, map VI

This flagged route is sufficiently difficult to follow that it is best termed a bushwhack. It was marked as a ski trail, but its slopes make it difficult even for snowshoeing. As a hiking route, it offers some surprisingly lovely views. The flagged, mile-long route forks southwest from the Elm Island trail (section 34). If you are climbing McGinn directly, note that the shortest approach to this intersection is 2.3 miles, beginning from Lake Adirondack Road. The flagging directs you up through a draw, which is ringed on the west by cliffs that gradually increase in height. Tumbled boulders litter their base. After about fifteen minutes, the route turns sharply right away

McGinn Mountain

from the cliffs and continues along a hog back. The slopes to your right become increasingly steep, and in less than ten minutes more you reach the first lookout southwest with Snowy in view. The route winds back beneath the steepest ledges, then out to another lookout on a narrow ledge. A third lookout gives views around to the southeast over the Siamese Ponds Wilderness. Forty-five minutes from the snowmobile trail, a sign, "Xpert Ski Trail to Summit," points to a cleft in the cliffs. Even in summer it is a fair scramble to climb west up to the summit, completing the bushwhack in about an hour.

The view from the summit offers a wide panorama to the south and east. At 2216 feet (681 meters) it provides one of the few lookouts in the area. The most prominent peak is Snowy Mountain, with Burgess Mountain closer to the right and Panther in the right background. To the right of these you can see Metcalf Mountain with Wakeley in the distance. To the west you can see the Blue Ridge Mountain with the Stark Hills in the foreground. On a clear day you can see the island-dotted water of Indian Lake fading off to the distant south. The peaks of the Siamese Ponds Wilderness stretch out to the east of it. To the far left the bare rocky face of Moxham rises in the distance.

36 Rock Lake and Rock River
Cross-country skiing, hiking, camping
3 miles one way, 1 hour and 20 minutes, 350-foot descent to the river, map VI

Two trails lead to Rock Lake, which is a mile-long oval bordered on the west by huge marshes. The south and eastern shores are dry and handsome with a number of good camping sites. The lake has become very popular in recent years though it is large enough to accommodate the current level of visitors. Fishing, birding, picnicking, boating are all delightful here.

The eastern trail only skirts the lake and continues on to a camping spot on Rock River. Near the river it intersects the snowmobile trail from Unknown Pond (section 33). A path leads west from the eastern trail along the southern shore of the lake. It intersects the western trail to the pond and is described in section 34. If you are out with a group of friends for a day's walk, I think the best way to sample the lake would be to make a loop with cars at either end, using the western trail, the path, and part of this trail.

The trail begins from a well-marked pullout on the north side of NY 30, 2.8 miles northwest of the bridge over the Cedar River. Snowmobile markers direct you through a second growth maturing forest with an open understory. The trail is generally north and soon heads fairly steeply downhill. (Skiers may find this stretch difficult.) Within twenty minutes, almost a mile from the highway, the descent ends, and you cross a small inlet stream on a bridge. The trail crosses a low rise and reaches a mucky area with corduroy. Just before the mucky area, there is a narrow, unmarked path that angles back to the left, west (see section 34).

The trail continues north, crosses a second small inlet, and circles around a small bay. This is the trail's closest approach to the lake. Next, the trail makes two jogs, sort of following the contour of the shoreline but well back from it, climbing away from lake level here. Yellow diamonds mark the trail where it crosses a flat area, 300 to 400 yards from the shore of the lake. Look closely, for there are several paths in this vicinity that lead from the trail to the best campsites along the shoreline. One is in the flat area at the tip of a small peninsula. Some of the shore is sandy, and most of the sites have lovely views across the lake to Blue Mountain.

Beyond the lake the trail, still winding north, contours around the lower slopes of the Stark Hills, a cone-shaped mountain whose southern flanks are ranked with cliffs and ledges. (If you are tempted, a mile-long, 500-foot bushwhack climb from the trail from this level area, east, then southeast, will take you to a vantage point on the cliffs of Stark Hills.)

The forest cover becomes more stately with large maples and birch giving way to towering hemlock. One hour and ten minutes from the road, about 2.6 miles, you reach a wet and confusing open area. An arrow directs you left through it. The way right is the snowmobile trail of section 39. A ten-minute, 0.4 mile, sharp descent takes you down to river level. Here is a wide-flowing quiet stream. A beaver dam holds back a large marsh bordered with alders upstream. You will find a camping spot on this side of the river and another handsome one across, which you can reach by hopping rocks in the stream—if the water is low.

37 Rock Lake

Marked trails, cross-country skiing, camping, hiking, fishing
0.75 mile, 15 minutes, level, 1.15-mile connector to eastern trail, 30 minutes, relatively level, maps VI, VII

The western trail to Rock Lake reaches the marshy southwestern corner of the lake from a marked trailhead, which is 1.4 miles west of the eastern trailhead. The wonderful smell of balsam distinguishes this route, which leads to an intersection near the Johnny Mack Brook inlet, 200 yards from the shore of the lake.

The trail continues north to lakeshore, winding through alder marshes and barely dry most of the year. The only justification for reaching the shore at this point in summer is that it is the shortest distance for carrying a canoe, and exploring the lake by canoe is most desirable. You will not find a dry spot to stand on, but you can briefly enjoy the view of Blue Mountain.

With a canoe you can watch birds in the western marshes and find the inlet, which winds through the northern marshes. The inlet is canoeable for nearly a mile upstream. Unfortunately, a long stretch of rapids separates the end of the canoeable stretch from a fifteen-foot waterfall well upstream. The pool where the river meets the lake is especially scenic. In late summer red maples blaze the shoreline.

If you are skiing and the lake is well frozen, you can easily explore the marshes as well as the rest of the shoreline. If you are on foot, cross the bridge over Johnny Mack Brook and continue east along the lake shore on the informal path. Huge pines cover several camping spots, all reached by short paths from the main route. A twenty-minute, 0.7-mile walk from the bridge takes you to a small stream that drains a large grassy marsh to the south. A new bridge of sorts lets you cross the marsh here. On the east you will find a faint path leading up and over a hemlock- and spruce-covered ledge. Another route circles below the ledge, bordering the northwest side of the marsh. Both paths intersect 200 yards west, below the knoll. The continuing path reaches the eastern trail to Rock Lake in 200 yards. (See section 36 for a description of that intersection should you wish to make the loop in the counterclockwise direction.)

38 Rock Lake to Lake Durant
Snowmobile trail
2.5 miles one way, 1 hour, maps VI, VII

A trail has been marked to lead from a point opposite the Lake Durant Campground entrance to Rock Lake. It generally follows the road and is not very exciting for other uses. It heads west from the Rock Lake Trail opposite the beginning of the south shore path. The first mile is a pleasant nature walk, circling a small hill and passing through fields of maidenhair, over hummocks in cedar swamps, and across sphagnum mats in spruce flats. This section reaches a point 200 yards from the highway at a path used by hunters to enter the woods west of Forest House. The continuing route is not far from the highway and too far from the river to be of interest to hikers, except those wishing to walk to Rock Lake from the Durant Lake Campground.

39 Rock River Loop
Snowmobile trail, long ski trip
8.7 miles, 5 to 6 hours, 300 feet elevation change, maps VI, VII

This loop combines the 2.3-mile ski to Unknown Pond (of section 33) and the 3-mile ski to the Rock River (section 36) with 3.4 miles of trail in the Rock River valley.

   Stay on the snowmobile trail as it descends to the marshes north of Unknown Pond. From this point the trail makes a large loop around the northern flanks of the Stark Hills. This segment is relatively little used by snowmobiles, particularly on weekdays, so skiing is pleasant. However, there are enough blowdowns to make skiing difficult. The trail winds northeast from the marshes by Unknown Pond for 0.8 mile to a footbridge at the edge of a second marsh. Actually, the entire area northeast of Unknown Pond is a series of marshes that provide habitat and nesting area for water-loving birds.

The trail heads north along the western edge of the second marsh, then curves west again to cross a bridge over a stream 2.2 miles from Unknown Pond. There is a third bridge 0.5 mile farther along, then an almost level traverse for 0.8 mile to intersect the Rock River Trail.

There is only a 70-foot difference between Unknown Pond and the intersection and although there are a number of gentle ups and downs, this is a remarkably level trail for its length. The only serious grade is the 250-foot climb to the highway at the end of the Rock River Trail. For skiing the loop, it might be better to leave a car at the landfill and make the trip from west to east. In summer there is little attraction in the middle portion of the trail, mostly because the best parts are more easily reached from either end point.

40 Tirrell Pond from the South
Marked trail, hiking, camping, cross-country skiing
4.6 miles to north end of pond, 2½ hours, 150 feet vertical rise, map VII

This is the easiest route to Tirrell Pond, which is an exceptional destination. The slides of Tirrell Mountain resemble those on Blue Mountain and form a handsome backdrop to this mile-long pond. The surrounding woods are fully mature and part of its shoreline is a marvel in the Adirondacks—sandy beaches are really a rarity. There are numerous campsites in addition to the two lean-tos. Fishing was always exceptional, and in spite of the numbers of campers, loons frequent the pond. In mid-week you can even join them in finding solitude here. However, the trail itself is of varied interest. Like many stretches of the Northville-Placid Trail, of which this is a portion, the trail passes through disturbed areas; half the route is on private land, which is logged.

The trail begins opposite the Lake Durant Campground and a large marked turnout. The trail climbs the banks beside the road and parallels the road for a short distance, then heads northeast. It keeps a course of east of north with a few small winding detours all the way to the pond. You wind across a small hill with gentle ups and downs to descend to a small, wet meadow. As you cross the meadow on a narrow corduroy bridge, you can see Blue Mountain across the flow to your left.

If you are hiking in summer, the numbers of mosquitoes that descend are good trail markers to the way the route now circles close to the western end of O'Neill Flow. Half an hour from the highway, at 1.4 miles, you reach a sign marking the posted lands of Finch Pruyn Company, which grants access north over their lands to Tirrell Pond.

At this point you cross a wet marsh and a stream that drains the marsh, which stretches west in a long, narrow flow. The stream crossing is on a new, raised bridge; the flow crossing is along a series of corduroy sections. Just beyond the crossing, look to your left, ahead. A big, syenite ledge faces the hillside and looks the same as the ledges on Blue Mountain that are visible from the highway.

The tote road origins of this portion of the trail are most obvious. Shortly beyond, you are at your closest approach to the flow though leaving the trail to look at it is disappointing. You would need elevation from which to look across the flow which extends east for more than a mile. The trail turns north into deeper woods, crosses a woods road, and continues as a narrow path through fields of brambles. Just short of 2 miles, a forty-five-minute hike, you cross an open meadow and then a little stream on a decrepit bridge.

You turn northwest to follow the stream and reach the 1883-foot benchmark 350 yards beyond. You cross two more streams before climbing to intersect a large woods road at right angles. The area has been logged fairly recently. For the next mile the trail is through these logged lands, following a fairly good dirt road. You will meet several side tracks, but trail marking is sufficient to keep you on the route although, at times, new growth in the openings might momentarily confuse the way.

A tenth of a mile from the lake, you reach the end of the private lands. The level stretch to the outlet of the pond takes you close to the O'Neill Lean-to. Cross the outlet to enjoy the view up the pond. This is a special place.

The 1.1-mile walk along the shore northwest to the Tirrell Pond Lean-to has had some recent trail work. It crosses several small streams and some wet areas and is presently acceptable. However, the new log work will soon deteriorate. This section needs rerouting to carry the number of people who use it. The trail is too far from the shore most of the time to give good views but too close to avoid the spruce flats that come right down to pond

Tirrell Pond Outlet

side. The cover makes this a handsome stretch, but the ground is no place for a trail.

Short of halfway along the pond, watch for a path that will take you to a sandy promontory, one of the prettier places along the shore. Remember, if you are camping anywhere along the pond, DEC regulations require you to be 150 feet back from the water.

41 Tirrell Pond from the West
Marked trail, hiking, camping
3.25 miles one way, 1½ hours, 500-foot descent, map VII

The shortest way to reach Tirrell Pond is via the red-marked trail from NY 30. It begins at the big, new, very popular trailhead at the height-of-land on NY 30 north of the Adirondack Museum at Blue Mountain Lake. The trail climbs gently for 100 feet, then descends gradually for 500 feet to pond level. Most of the route is over private lands and through disturbed forests.

The trail leaves the north end of the parking area and parallels the road briefly before heading northeast to contour around Blue Mountain on an old tote road. After thirty-five minutes, at 1.6 miles, you cross a stream and a private roadway which heads up the mountain. Beyond the roadway, a second stream, this one rusty with iron oxides, is followed by a succession of small streams that drain the mountain.

After forty-five minutes, you reach a private-land sign. Wet places in the trail follow, then you begin to descend in an easterly direction through the draw between Blue Mountain and Buck Mountain to the north. Where logging roads cross the trail, watch for signs to keep you on the correct route.

An hour and a half from the highway, and less than 0.5 mile from the pond, you reach state land. A stream appears on your right and you follow it briefly, then cross it. Just beyond is the intersection with the blue-marked Northville-Placid Trail. Follow this southeast for another five minutes to cross another stream. Already you can see the pond through the trees. For a description of the pond and a walk along its southern shore see section 40.

Tirrell Pond

42 Blue Mountain
Marked trail, hiking, views
5 miles round trip, 3½ hours, 1516 feet (474 meters) vertical rise, map VII

Blue Mountain's elevation, 3667 feet (1146 meters), and its location in the center of the Adirondacks—isolated from other mountains—made it ideal for the surveyor Verplanck Colvin, who made it one of his key triangulation points. In his report to the legislature of his *Topographical Survey of the Adirondack Region*, he refers to Blue Mountain by the name Mount Emmons, after the earlier Adirondack surveyor.

In 1876 Colvin made his third and fourth ascents of the mountain, the fourth on a horse that could not navigate the descent over the rough trail Colvin's assistants had cut to the summit.

Past the halfway point on the climb, try to imagine what it would have been like to try to make a trail through the spruce and balsam and the deadfalls and over ledges on the mountain's western flank. Colvin's assistants and guides had cut the trail so they could carry his surveying equipment to the summit, principally a large theodolite which he used to determine the heights of other key mountains. They also cleared the northern summit so mountains to the west, north and east were visible. Colvin established camp on the summit, had a small log cabin built, and arranged for signal flashes to be set off each clear evening at 9:00 P.M.

These flashes continued during the summer months for the next several years while he was completing his survey of the Adirondacks.

Colvin knew Blue Mountain Lake as Tallow Lake. The region around the lake grew quickly into one of the Adirondacks' most sumptuous resorts. Colvin observed in 1878 that

> where in 1870 and '73, the small bark shanty of our hunter guide stood solitary—our only shelter—near the sand beaches of Blue Mountain Lake, now stand here and there the comfortable woodland hotels, with semi-rustic grounds, and bright Concord coaches, drawn by sleek 'four' or 'six-n-hands,' lend color to the scene. Yet the boat-canoes that cluster on the sand beach, mutely but eloquently, tell of the sweet corners which may be reached in them, not only on these lakes, but more distant waters.

Blue Mountain is so special and so many people have discovered how wonderful it is, that the best guide to it begins with the advice not only to pick a clear day, but to start out very early in the morning or in late afternoon, preferably mid-week. The newly rerouted beginning of the trail avoids the private land problems of the old trailhead. The new route leaves from the parking area at the height-of-land, north of the Adirondack Museum on NY 30.

The trail heads east from the parking area, following a logging road for 300 yards to a sign-in booth. The land on both sides here is posted. You cross a small stream on a half-log bridge, then begin a fairly steep climb. The trail is already rutted and worn, exposing roots and rocks that make the going rough.

A twenty-minute, 0.6-mile climb, leads to a level stretch with two small streams to cross. Then the trail turns southeast to begin a steep traverse that ends, at 1.5 miles after a 600-foot, forty-minute climb, at another stream crossing. A short, steep 100-yard pitch takes you to the intersection with the old trail.

The steepest part of the climb begins immediately. Thousands of feet have worn the trail to bedrock so that you climb up slabs like paving or pick your way around rocks and boulders for most of the rest of the climb. The route is due east for 0.5 mile, then heads northeast. The last few hundred yards are across a level ridge through sphagnum mats that are bridged by sections of corduroy.

There is often a waiting line for the climb to the tower on clear weekends. Even if you find many other hikers on the summit, you can find openings to the east and north in the spruce-covered summit. Rock perches provide quiet picnic spots.

43 East Inlet Brook
Bushwhack, map IX

Most of both sides of the road along NY 30 from Blue Mountain Lake to Long Lake is privately owned. The only state land access is along an old tote road that follows East Inlet Brook into the valley toward Mt. Sabattis. The tote road will get you to the brook, but it quickly disappears so any further travel is a bushwhack along the brook.

NY 30 crosses a marshy area 6.7 miles north of the Adirondack Museum, 1.4 miles south of the intersection with the North Point Road to the Raquette River at Deerland. North of the marsh there is a field on the west side of the road which has been used to store vehicles for the recent NY 30 reconstruction. Across the road opposite the field, there is an almost-concealed dirt track. It heads west around the marshes that here surround the brook. Several beaver dams enlarge the wetlands around the brook.

After the track crosses a small stream on an old bridge, the way becomes increasingly obscured by new growth of small spruce. You can fight through the spruce and reach the stream above the marshes. Cascades and small waterfalls mark the stream as it rises to the northeast, ever more steeply through the narrowing valley. However, no discernible route except the course of the brook guides you further.

West of Blue Mountain and Long Lakes

WEST OF LONG and Blue Mountain lakes is a region of lakes, spruce flats, bogs, and relatively level terrain. It is bounded on the south by the Eckford Chain of Lakes and the Marion River and on the west by Raquette Lake. Travel by water to the region's periphery has been so easy that the interior trails are not heavily used.

Because this is a designated Wild Forest Area, float planes can land on the two major interior attractions, the Upper and Lower Sargent Ponds. As a result, there are a lot of fishermen who camp at the lakes in the spring, but few people walk to them in summer even though the trails are in good condition.

Almost every visitor to the area drives south along North Point Road from Deerland to visit Buttermilk Falls on the Raquette River. North Point Road, County Road 3, intersects NY 30 7.7 miles north of Blue Mountain Lake and 3 miles south of Long Lake Village. The falls is 2.1 miles southwest of NY 30 and a perfect place for a picnic.

When William H. H. (Adirondack) Murray wrote his *Adventures in the Wilderness*, the first book to popularize the Adirondacks, he embellished his description of the wilds with a few fancy tales. The most famous was told to him by his guide, the trapper John Norton. Over a campfire near the falls, John told of Wisti, the daughter of a Huron chief, who fell in love with a Jesuit priest. The priest returned to Montreal to ask to be released from his vows but never came back as promised to meet her at the falls. She regularly visited the falls at dusk, and one day, perhaps in despair, she was swept over them. Her ghost continued to return to the spot. John claimed to have seen the phantom, and his fireside story telling was so vivid, Murray saw it, too. According to Murray, they set out in a canoe to pursue the apparition and ended up chasing it down river until they, too, were swept over the "Phantom Falls."

South Pond

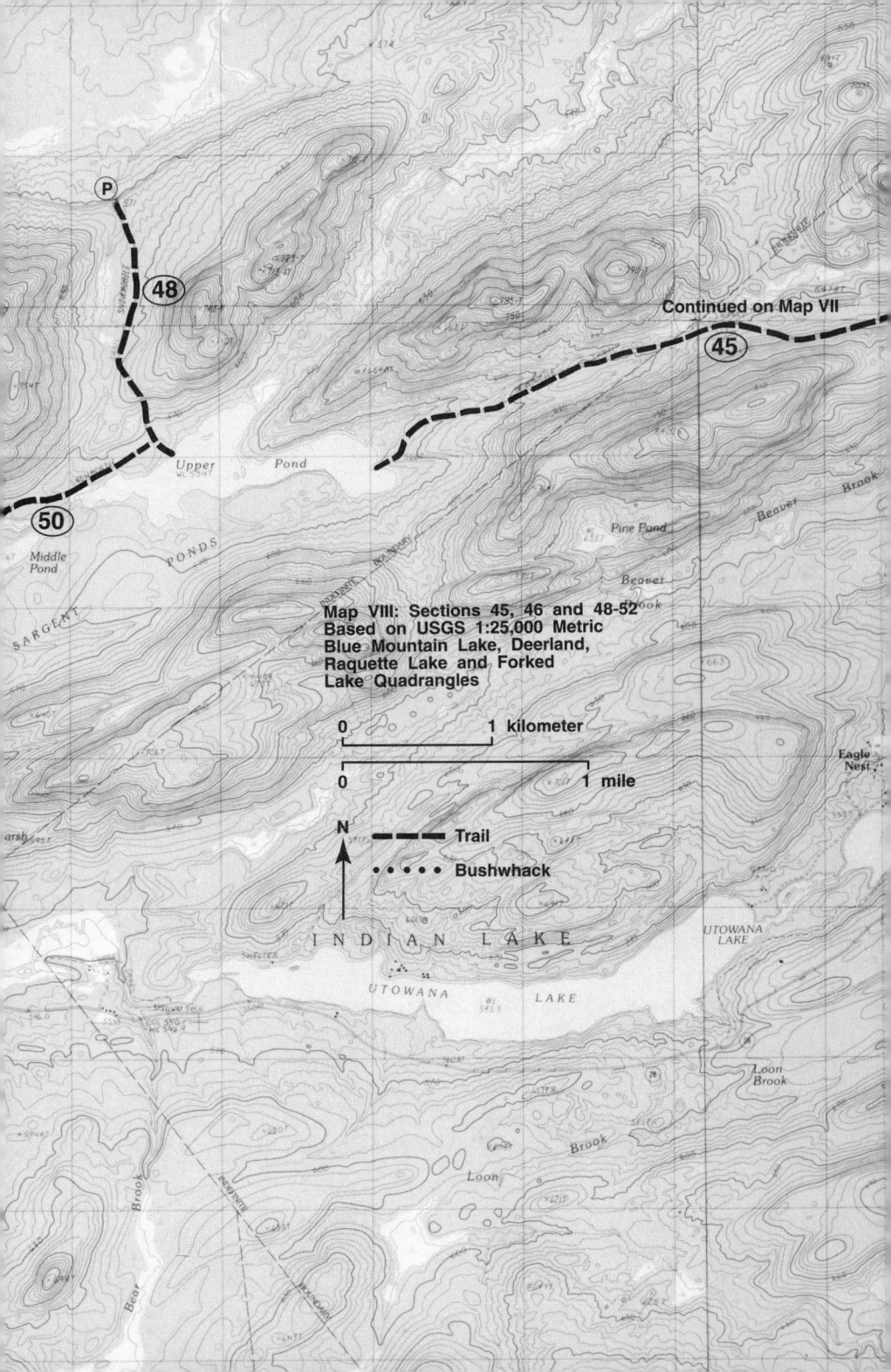

From Castle Rock

44 Castle Rock
Short hike, view, picnicking
1.8 miles one way, under an hour, 420-foot climb, map VII

A steep, jagged rock peak rises above the north shore of island-studded Blue Mountain Lake. This sheer face of granite gneiss towers over 500 feet above the lake. A climb to the top of the rock ledges will give you breathtaking views: the entire lake spreads out shimmering beneath you with Blue Ridge Mountain dominating the skyline just west of south; to the left, the towering mass of Blue Mountain is framed by red spruce; further around to the left, Minnow Pond nestles in a hollow; to the right, Helms Pond can be seen below Little Blue Mountain; and many peaks can be identified in the distant southern panorama.

To reach Castle Rock, you drive north on NY 30 for 0.6 mile from the intersection of NY 30 and NY 8 at Blue Mountain Lake. Turn left on Maple Lodge Road, where a sign indicates Minnowbrook Conference Center, and drive 1.5 miles to the end. Here a DEC sign indicates the trail to Upper Sargent Pond, and another indicates that no motorized vehicles are permitted beyond this point. Park carefully at the side of the road in a way that does not block side roads and driveways. A good parking area is needed here.

The beginning of the trail is a continuing roadway on private land, which can be crossed without asking permission. Follow the main dirt road as it heads west, angles up a hill, and then swings right in a loop. The hiking trail with red markers begins on the right just before a bridge over the outlet of Chub Pond. The route, generally north at first, is well used and marked. It can be skied or snowshoed in the winter although there are one or two blowdowns which must be avoided. After crossing the outlet of Minnow Pond, the trail climbs fairly steeply and curves around to the west. After crossing two more small streams, the trail crosses a slightly larger stream and, at 1.1 miles, enters a clearing with the remains of a small well.

Continuing upgrade not far from the stream, within ten minutes, at 1.4 miles, you will see a rock cairn on the left of the trail and a large forked yellow birch with two red disks. Look left for a straight yellow-blazed trail, which leads to Castle Rock.

Follow this trail in a curving arc to the southwest, climbing gradually. As you reach the ridge and begin to wind around to the south, the area is quite damp; and most of the trees are dead. Beneath the jumble of deadwood there is a fantastic variety of mosses on the moist rocks. Christmas fern and spinulose woodfern poke through the lingering snow and edge the small brooks.

As you follow the yellow blazes up and around to the south side of the peak, you may note a red-blazed trail joining your route. At this point, you turn left, east, to climb steeply, but easily, up the last 100 feet to the top of the rock.

On your return, after you drop down from the knob, be sure to turn right to retrace your steps on the yellow trail. The red-marked route to the left leads to private land with no public access.

45 Blue Mountain Lake to Upper Sargent Pond

Hiking, cross-country skiing, camping, fishing
4.8 miles one way, 2¼ hours, minimal elevation change, maps VII, VIII

The beginning of this marked DEC trail coincides with the beginning of the trip to Castle Rock (section 44). Start on the private road, turn onto the well-marked (red disks) hiking trail, and continue past the fork to the Castle Rock Trail at 1.8 miles.

You cross several small streams; all are passable by hopping rocks. The trail heads west, with relatively little change in elevation. After an hour's walk, about 0.4 mile past the fork to Castle Rock, Helms Pond is in a valley on your right, north, but invisible. In the spring or fall you can see the rocky western bluff of Little Blue Mountain above it. The trail continues up and down small hills, heading generally south of west. It is an open, gradual trail with a number of wet spots in the spring. When there is enough snow to cover the rocks and cold weather to make the small streams passable, this is a fine cross-country ski trail.

The trail is south of the valley of Helms Pond Outlet and the flows and marshes that surround it. On the higher ground to the left are large, irregular boulders which look like natural bear dens. The trail gradually moves down slope, reaching valley level at 3.2 miles and staying close to the outlet for the remaining 1.6 miles downhill to the pond.

After about two hours, you see a part of Upper Sargent Pond to the right; the trail avoids the swampy outlet of the pond and leads left, down a slope to an attractive spruce- and balsam-forested point. A large, but neat, hunter's camp is hidden among the trees. Walk cautiously to the water's edge for you may surprise an otter. Wood ducks frequent the bay. Sheep laurel thrives in crevices of the large smooth rocks on the point. The irregular tree-lined shores of this pond are always pleasant and relaxing.

This is the end of the trail in summer, but in winter you can ski west down the shoreline to the trail which comes in from North Point Road. If you leave a shuttle car on the latter road, this makes an easy seven-mile ski trip on clear, marked trails. Alternatively, you could reverse the route as there is a DEC sign on the point which locates the trail back to Blue Mountain Lake.

The hike back, where you will notice that the route is slightly uphill, also takes just over two hours.

46 Lower Sargent Pond from Marion River Carry
Path, hiking, fishing
1 mile (after a canoe trip), ½ hour, relatively level, map VIII

Older topographic maps showed a traditional path from the Marion River Carry beside NY 28 to Lower Sargent Pond. In fact, this is not a feasible route as it begins on posted, private land. Furthermore, the part of the old path on state land has not been used, is blocked by many blowdowns, crisscrossed by hunter and animal paths, and, essentially, is impossible to follow.

This section describes an alternate path on public land that has been worn by fishermen and hikers, but the beginning can be reached only by water from the Marion River. The usual access is up the Marion River from Raquette Lake. About three-quarters of the way from the lake to the canoe carry, there is a pine tree (the only one) over the river on the north side at a landing.

Take your canoe out here and look for the beginning of the unmarked path to Lower Sargent Pond. The mile-long path begins here and winds generally north, rising from 1800 to 1840 feet, staying well to the west of Haymarsh Pond. Turn right, east, to the pond which you will soon glimpse through the trees. There is a pleasant dry place to camp back from the shore; a sand beach invites you to a cool swim.

A different way to reach the beginning of the path is a portage along Marion River Carry and a paddle downstream to the landing by the pine tree. To reach the "carry," drive west from the village of Blue Mountain Lake on NY 28 for 6.3 miles. There is a cable visible from the road across a path which goes north down to the west end of Lake Utowana, just above the dam which marks the beginning of the Marion River. The path is marked for canoe access to the Marion River. Carry your canoe to the lake (100 yards), and paddle the short distance across (100 feet). Now portage your canoe downstream, west, beside the Marion River rapids—a ten-minute walk to where the river widens and levels out. Pause about two-thirds of the way down this portage to admire the large bed of trailing arbutus. In spring its beautiful pink and white flowers and exquisite fragrance explain the plant's popularity and the necessity for protecting it. When you reach the wide section of stream, paddle downstream about 0.7 mile and land by the pine tree on the north bank.

The Marion River Carry has a unique and historic past. As you dock your canoe after paddling across Lake Utowana, you will be surprised to see a pile of rotting timbers—the remains of a steamship dock. If you look close while portaging, you will see the remains of railroad tracks. You are walking along the bed of the shortest standard gauge railway to operate in the world. In the late 1800s steamers plied the waters of both Raquette Lake and Blue Mountain Lake bringing summer tourists to the resort hotels. The Bassett Carry, as it was then called, had a team of horses transferring people and their baggage along this stretch through the 1890s. William West Durant saw the need for eliminating the Bassett Carry bottleneck and constructed a 0.85-mile railroad from the dock on the

Marion River to the eastern terminus on Lake Utowana. People were met there by the steamboat Utowana, or one of two others which were built later, and were taken up through Lake Utowana, Eagle Lake, and into Blue Mountain Lake and the steamboat landing. The railroad ran from 1920 until September 15, 1929. During most of its operation this short line had the wealthiest Board of Directors ever assembled: W. Seward Webb, J. Pierpont Morgan, Harry P. Whitney, Reginald C. Vanderbilt, and William Hamilton. These indeed were the "heydays" of the Adirondacks. You should combine a visit to the carry with a trip to the Adirondack Museum where you can see the railroad cars and many photographs of those exciting times.

47 South Pond
Canoeing, picnicking, map IX

One of the most memorable and enjoyable days that you can spend on flat water is paddling a canoe on South Pond. Although it is near the road (NY 30) and there are private camps on the northwest shore and along one side of the southeast bay, there are many rocky islands and sheltered bays for exploring or camping. The private land is conspicuously posted, and most of the shoreline is state land. This body of water is large enough—it is really a lake, so you can explore serenely, particularly on weekdays or during the fall.

If you are a bird lover, you are in for a thrill. Take binoculars and a picnic lunch to eat on one of the islands, all of which are state land; nearly a dozen are scattered in the south portion of the pond. Watch for loons which will swim and dive as they feed. One island has an osprey nest in the top of a tall pine. Do not land on that island, but appreciate it from a distance, especially if the birds are nesting. You can land on most of the small islands, but on weekends in summer you may find someone is already there. And the smallest islands—the ones that are no more than a cluster of rocks—are often home to nesting sea gulls.

The pond is deep with rock outcrops along the shoreline. The shores of the islands are covered with viburnums and hollies. Paddle to the southeast to the marshes along the outlet to see Labrador tea and other water-loving shrubs. Large floating mats of sphagnum lie just beneath the surface of the water along many parts of the lake, tangling your paddle as you dock.

It is easy to reach South Pond by car; take NY 30 north from Blue Mountain Lake for 5.9 miles to a turnout on the left, west, side of the road. The lake can be seen from the parking area, down the hill through the trees, 200 yards away. You can reach the pond by heading steeply downhill from the turnout; but if you walk to the north end of the turnout, there is a dirt track that provides an easier access. There are several places along the shore to launch and load a canoe; just to the south of the launch points there is a tiny cove with a lovely sand beach. As you paddle out, be careful to note the shoreline where you put in so that you can find it easily when you leave. The road is not visible from the pond.

48 Upper Sargent Pond from the North

Marked trail, hiking, camping, snowshoeing, cross-country skiing, fishing
1.3 miles, ½ hour one way, minimal elevation change, map VIII

To reach the trailhead for Upper Sargent Ponds, drive down North Point Road past Buttermilk Falls to a fork where you turn left. The right fork goes to the DEC Forked Lake Campground, a fine place to stay if you plan to hike in this vicinity. In winter the Long Lake Fish and Game Club uses this spur as a deer-feeding area. Driving slowly down this road in winter you are sure to see many deer.

The Lower Sargent Pond trailhead is 6.3 miles from NY 30 on the left fork. The trail is marked with both orange snowmobile disks and red hiking trail markers. It heads south rising slightly to a plateau with impressive yellow birch. A marsh to your right is filling in with evergreens. Climbing around the nose of a hill, then descending with a heading of east of south, the trail comes to an intersection, less than thirty minutes from the trailhead. The way left leads to Upper Sargent Pond. Continue straight ahead for two minutes to drop down through a hemlock grove to a campsite on a knoll at pondside. There is an island off to your left (summer hikers often swim to it) and two more islands concealing the entrance to the pond's eastern lobe. The pond is long and thin and irregularly shaped with many bays. You really need a boat to explore it; and even if it seems too far for carrying a canoe, a rubber raft will do.

Paddling the deep bays and secluded coves is delightful. The banks are less dense than the other ponds although spruce-fir growth can be seen along much of the shoreline. Hunters fly in to the pond in the fall when the campsite is heavily used. If you ski in during winter, you can easily ski to the western end where the view east is especially beautiful. Two unnamed mountains form a sharp V in the distance.

49 Lower Sargent Pond via Grass Pond
Marked trail, hiking, camping, snowshoeing, cross-country skiing, fishing
2.1 miles, 1¼ hours, minimal elevation change, map VIII

The trailhead for Lower Sargent Pond is 1.6 miles east of the Upper Pond trailhead or 7.9 miles from NY 30. The trail has both orange snowmobile trail markers and red hiking trail markers. The trail starts at 1780 feet and rises very gradually, heading south through an old growth forest. Very large yellow birch, beech, and hemlock with occasional young balsam flank the open trail which courses up and down crossing small watercourses.

Because snowmobile use is light, you can ski this route, with caution, but note that the snowmobiles create hummocks on the trail and sharp dips in the gullies. You may find it easier to ski in the virgin snow beside the trail and zigzag across the sharp depressions.

The trail takes you gently up and across high ground, then south beside Grass Pond. Beaver flooding has forced the trail to arc west, then it drops to the marsh at the head of the pond at 1.3 miles, a half-hour walk, longer on skis. The pond is shallow and marshy at the northern end though there are large white pines back from the shore of the pond. A large spruce stand graces the southwest shore.

Continuing south beside the marshy inlet stream, the trail quickly reaches high ground again. After traversing a tall forest of maple and yellow birch—some of the largest you will see anywhere—and curving southeast, the trail reaches an intersection at 2 miles, less than twenty minutes from Grass Pond. One sign points south to Lower Sargent Pond, .1 mile, and Tioga Point 3.5 miles. Another sign points northeast to Upper Sargent Pond, 1.7 miles. You continue south through a wet area with blowdowns; you cross two plank bridges wide enough for snowmobiles; and soon you see the pond.

You reach Lower Sargent Pond at a fish barrier dam which is designed to prevent upstream migration of unwanted species. The main trail goes to the right across the outlet and continues to Tioga Point (section 51).

West of Blue Mountain Lake   115

There is a left fork to the east which circles a stand of spruce to reach a lean-to on a pine-covered point on the north shore of the pond. In winter you can cut immediately through the spruce- and balsam-thicket and go out onto the pond.

Lower Sargent Pond is a round, deep, 134-acre body of water at 1754 feet elevation. The west and north shores are rimmed by an esker of sand, gravel, and rock about five to six feet high and averaging ten feet in width. Tall white pines grow majestically on this lip of earth. Behind them, away from the pond but at the same level as the pond, is found a moist area thickly covered by spruce and fir. The ecological contrast of the forest communities is striking.

Because this lower pond is a popular fly-in for several commercial air services, there might be 15 to 20 boats on the water at one time in the spring. The best camping site is at the lean-to, but there are other sites around the shore. If the pond is not crowded, this is a grand place to spend a few days fishing and swimming—there is even an aluminum boat on shore in front of the lean-to.

50 Sargent Ponds Loop via Middle Pond
Marked trail, skiing, hiking, camping, fishing
6.9-mile loop, 5 hours, minimal elevation change, map VIII

This 6.9-mile loop is a delight to ski, with two legs the trips to the Upper and Lower Sargent Ponds (sections 48 and 49) and a third leg, the 1.6 miles between the trailheads along North Point Road. (With two cars, this stretch can be eliminated; but since the circuit is so short, that is not really necessary.) The fourth leg is a 1.7 mile trip between the ponds (both of whose end-points are described in the sections above). Your route between the ponds will vary depending on the season.

In winter you can either ski or snowshoe to the northeast corner of the pond and bushwhack up a slight hill to Middle Sargent Pond. You ski across its long axis in the same east-northeasterly direction and make your way through a dense stand of spruce and fir. Soon you climb out of the flat up a slope of mixed hardwoods and hemlocks, then down a long gentle hill onto Upper Sargent Pond. With the exception of the spruce flats near Middle Sargent Pond, the forest is open enough to permit skiing.

Alternatively, in winter you could follow the marked snowmobile trail which stays well to the north of Middle Sargent Pond, avoiding the spruce

116 Discover the Central Adirondacks

which line its northern shore. Because snowmobile use is so light on these trails, you can, with caution, ski the stretch between the ponds. However, this way you will miss Middle Sargent Pond since the trail is 200 to 300 yards north of it, away from the spruce flats and along a hardwood ridge.

In summer you would follow the marked snowmobile trail for all of this leg, missing Middle Sargent Pond. Even missing Middle Sargent Pond, you will find few loops this short have so many views of different ponds and such a diversity of forest cover.

51 Tioga Point to Lower Sargent Pond
Hiking, fishing, camping, cross-country skiing
4 miles one way, 2 hours, minimal elevation change, map VIII

Trails reach the three Sargent Ponds from all points of the compass, and each route traverses a different forest type. This western route begins at Tioga Point, the western tip of this guidebook, which lies on Raquette Lake. You can reach Tioga Point only by water, unless you walk, ski, or snowmobile in from the east using this route.

In 1877, Ike Kenwell opened a hotel known as the Raquette Lake House. It burned in 1887 and was not rebuilt, but you can see the large stone chimney with its double fireplace which still stands on the flat, pine-covered point. Today there are fifteen open shelters for camping on the point. Reservations for them can be made through the DEC Reservation System although except in summer and early fall they may not be necessary. The campground is a popular place in summer because it lies on the heavily traveled canoe routes from the Fulton Chain through Raquette Lake to the north.

To reach Tioga Point by canoe, put your canoe in at the public launch site in the hamlet of Raquette Lake, which is one mile off NY 28, or drive all the way through town to Forest Preserve land on Lonesome Bay north of Antlers Point. From the public dock to Tioga Point is about a three-mile paddle up and across the lake. The trailhead for the snowmobile and hiking trail to Lower Sargent Pond begins from the northeast corner of the open fields behind Tioga Point.

There is considerable discrepancy in the signs for this trail. Here the distance to the pond is given as 2.8 miles with 5 miles to North Point Road. At the North Point Road end, the distance grows to 5.5 miles, with

Tioga Point

3.4 being allotted to the Tioga Point-Lower Sargent Pond portion. The through trek is actually 6.5 miles, 2.1 from North Point Road to the pond, 0.4 around the pond, and the 4-mile segment described here.

Walk east on the marked snowmobile trail which occasionally has yellow hiking trail disks as well. The tall white pine forest quickly gives way to smaller red pine. As you move to higher ground, you reach an open hardwood forest with many large, old trees decaying on the forest floor. Moss-covered logs beside the trail bear beautiful fungus, including the shiny maroon-colored *Ganoderum lucidum*.

The open trail winds around and down a small hill; Eldon Lake, a bay of Raquette Lake, can be seen through the trees on the right. There are several more primitive campsites along that shore—unofficial—but well-used. After a half-hour walk you are opposite the head of Eldon Lake, and just beyond it a cairn marks a fork right for a two-minute walk to a pine-covered knoll at the head of the bay. Look for an osprey on the top of the majestic white pines that grow from hummocks in the marshy area to the south of the trail.

At 1.8 miles, you cross a small brook and a marshy area. Here the trailside changes to the boreal plants of the north woods spruce swamps. The forest floor is densely covered with dryopteris species, the woodferns, and club mosses. Labrador tea likes this marshy place. Crush a leaf between your fingers to savor its pleasant aroma.

Beyond, the trail moves to higher and dryer ground with open mixed hardwoods that are great for deer hunting because of the limited undergrowth. Towering yellow birch rise skyward with gnarled scraggly topknot branches sheltering large forest openings around their trunks. Both standing and decaying trees nurture myriad fungus—perhaps this should be billed as a fungus walk. The artist's fungus grows profusely.

After an hour and a half, at about 3 miles, you come to a brook flowing north, a tributary of Boulder Brook. From here it is less than a mile, under thirty minutes, to the pond. Hardwoods continue all the way—open easy walking with no blowdowns. This makes it an excellent, easy cross-country ski trail, especially when packed by snowmobiles although few of them use this route and, then, primarily on weekends.

An unmarked path forks right to the shore of the pond, and you could follow on around the southwest shore to the unmarked path from the Marion River (section 46). Beyond, the snowmobile trail turns north and runs parallel to, but about 100 yards away from, the western shoreline. If you stay on it, you cross the outlet of the pond and can go out to the North Point Road (section 49) or continue to Upper Sargent Pond (section 50).

At this junction, a path leads straight downslope, east, to the pond and a nice sandy beach. Lower Sargent Pond has all the markings of a kettle pond, one which was formed when glacial ice was buried by the glacial till and outwash. When the ice melted, a sandy rim was left around the edge of the pond. There is a good camping spot back from the shore.

Do not be surprised to see canoes on the point from ice-out in mid-April until the end of fishing season. The pond is stocked with trout, and the fishing is good. Because of the area's Wild Forest designation, commercial seaplane operators regularly fly fishermen in with their canoes and camping gear.

The return to Tioga Point takes under two hours. As you canoe back across Raquette Lake, enjoy the views of Blue Mountain which towers majestically to the east, a giant overshadowing the lowlands, which border the lake. Alternately, you can make the trek in the opposite direction, considering this trail part of a 6.5-mile approach to Tioga Point from North Point Road.

52 Forked Lake
Camping, canoeing, swimming, map VIII

If you continue west on North Point Road past the Sargent Ponds trailheads, for a total of 9.1 miles west-southwest of NY 30, a dirt road forks right shortly after you cross the Raquette River. There is a "canoe carry" sign. The road is a portage from Raquette Lake to Forked Lake. You can drive down this road to the shore of Forked Lake. Unload canoe and gear beside the roofed cement dock and then drive your car back up the hill 100 yards to the designated visitors parking spot. (This is private land, open to the public through a special arrangement; so do not abuse it.)

Most of the shoreline and the islands of Forked Lake are privately owned and posted but two sections, in addition to the DEC public campground on the eastern bay, are state owned. You can reach either of them with a paddle of a mile or so.

If you paddle east from the dock along the cedar-rimmed shoreline, you will enjoy the esthetic experience of a sculpture garden formed by the upturned cedar roots in all sizes and shapes. When you see no more posted signs, look for open areas behind the cedar and places to land your canoe. There are several sites which previously had tent platforms, where you will find the concrete pillars and tumbled remains of wood sheds. The shore in this section has several kinds of water lilies. Look especially for a small floating plant with descriptive leaves and minute white flowers—floating hearts.

The other portion of state land is at the far western end of the lake. On the way there you will pass several small islands. Part of the shoreline is dominated by rock ledges. Most of the shore, however, is ringed by cedar which is neatly trimmed to about six feet above water level. This is the browse line of white-tailed deer who, when the lake is frozen, feed off the succulent leaves and twigs of this white cedar.

Paddle through a narrow section of the bay—somewhat tedious if the wind is from the west—and bear right. The first campsite is at a flat open area with a very rudimentary dock made by fishermen and hunters who often camp here. The other four sites at which to pitch a tent are farther along the same shoreline. There are also several campsites directly across the bay, up the slope in the woods away from the shore. A smooth-cobbled beach makes good access for swimming. Trout and perch can be caught by trolling. Loons frequently feed in this bay, and their calls at night are particularly clear and frequent. Bring binoculars to watch their springtime display.

At the end of the bay, pickerel weed carpets shallow coves, and fragrant water lilies and floating hearts abound. A quiet evening paddle in this cove is likely to surprise a beaver; you may not know he is there until you hear the tremendous swat as his tail hits the water. A half day or more can be spent exploring the entrance brook which meanders into Forked Lake from Brandreth Lake. Many varieties of bog plants can be found from the canoe: erect pitcher plants, green- and wine-colored in summer, bronze in fall; diminutive sundews with tendrils attracting insects to their sticky leaves; bunches of burreed with their ball-like heads of tiny green flowers; pink-flowered swamp rose mallow; underwater grasses floating ethereally in the current. Stark tamarack grow out of the marsh, framed by silvered cedar roots. Carry over the first beaver dam, and the next, and on! Great blue heron stand motionlessly in the shallows of the beaver ponds; kingfisher fly away with a loud rattling cry. A short, wet trail to the left provides a carry around a small rapids. Every turn brings a new view, eliciting a breath of beauty. There is something awe-inspiring about this sparse, marshy, bleak area. A day in this isolated inlet, working your canoe up as far as you can go before reaching private land, will give you a new perspective on the beauty and importance of such a marshy area.

Waterfall on Owl Mountain Pond Outlet

53 Owls Head Mountain and Lake Eaton

Hiking, snowshoeing, swimming
3.2 miles, 2 hours, 1140 feet (357 meters) vertical rise, red markers, map IX

Owls Head Mountain, elevation 2742 feet (857 meters), overlooks the lowlands that slope off to the Raquette River. Its view east surveys the Fishing Brook Range, with glimpses of the High Peaks beyond. It is an old fire-tower mountain; the tower stands with its lower staircases removed.

To reach the trailhead, drive through the village and north over the bridge over Long Lake. The first left turn, Endion Road, winds back south along the lake, serving cottages on the west shore. The trailhead, at 1.6 miles from NY 30, has signs pointing 4.8 miles to Lake Eaton Campground, 4.5 miles to NY 30, 3.1 miles to Owls Head Mountain, and 9.2 miles to Forked Lake. The latter refers to the abandoned and overgrown snowmobile trail that can no longer be used.

The trail heads uphill to a register, then climbs steeply to a height-of-land. At 0.5 mile, a snowmobile connector forks back right. The hiking trail and the snowmobile trail interweave in a westerly course. At 1 mile, there is a three-way intersection, the way right is one of two intersections that fork north toward Lake Eaton. The second fork toward Lake Eaton is 200 yards farther along on the left branch. Just beyond this, the abandoned Forked Lake Trail is a left fork. Here, stay straight; there are only red markers, no more snowmobile markers from this point on the Owls Head Mountain Trail.

The red trail continues fairly level for another 0.5 mile, then begins to climb gently at first. At 2.3 miles, the trail swings sharply south and becomes quite steep as it follows a brook that drains the draw between two of Owls Head's knobs. After crossing the saddle between the knobs, the trail descends at 3 miles to the site of the fire observer's cabin, today a small flower-filled meadow. The trail climbs Owls Head's southern knob in 0.2 mile, a steep route with rock stairs. This leads directly to the open rock below the tower.

On the return, take one of the two forks north toward Lake Eaton. They join in 0.2 mile and lead to shore in a sandy bay 0.4 mile from the red trail. The bay is a good place for a cooling swim. The snowmobile trail continues left here to circle around the lake to the campground or back out to NY 30, where snowmobile trails on the east side of NY 30 lead back toward Long Lake Village. Midweek, this complex of trails circling Lake Eaton make great skiing, but they are heavily used by the machines on most weekends.

54 Owls Head Pond
Difficult bushwhack, map IX

This bushwhack can be very difficult, in spite of the fact that part of the route is marked or flagged. Owls Head Pond is a delightful destination, a teardrop beneath Owls Head Mountain that appears like a dark pearl from that summit. Two routes are described.

To reach the beginning of the bushwhack it is necessary to canoe north along Long Lake narrows from the launch at the canoe carry, 1.8 miles south of NY 30 at Deerland. The carry is a 0.15-mile descent from North Point Road. Paddle north past two headlands on the west, each with rocks sloping to water level. Past the second the western shore opens to a broad marsh that surrounds Owls Head Pond Outlet. Paddle up that outlet to the first beaver dam and pull your canoe out here after about half an hour on the water. Walk upstream along the outlet. There is something of a path. In five minutes you reach a lovely waterfall. Upstream the outlet flows through a long, thin beaver marsh. When the stream climbs again, there are pretty rapids and small cascades, then a second marsh. Watch for a truly enormous pine. More marshes are followed by a small waterfall, then a steep, moss-covered bank. At this point, about 1.2 miles and fifty minutes from the start, watch for a washed-out snowmobile bridge that is lodged on the far shore of the diminishing stream. Two minutes upstream from it is the old crossing of the abandoned snowmobile trail, where the bridge ought to be. Red flags may help you find the trail, which is still obvious.

Owls Head Pond is only 0.5 mile away. To cross the outlet stream you have to go downstream to find rocks to hop on, and it may not be easy to find the continuing trail on the opposite bank. The trail winds through a marshy area to a second bridge, this one intact, over a small stream. Just across the bridge, turn left, heading just south of west and continue on a relatively level course in this direction. There may be red flags to guide you. The course hugs the steep base of the mountain to the north—its lower flanks covered with low cliffs. Hugging these slopes and climbing over a low ridge, your route gradually swings to north of west. In less than half an hour you sense an opening to the northwest. Climb the slopes and marvel at finding the pond in the middle of nowhere.

Be aware that the area south of the pond and its outlet streams is no place to wander about. Very small changes in contours, spruce swamps, and tiny wandering streams make it very confusing. You cannot follow the outlet to the pond because it loops south through the swamps.

Actually, the pond has had two outlets in the past. You come to the log-

Owl Mountain Pond

filled bay with the first outlet just after reaching the pond. Continue on west, across the base of a peninsula to the second bay, this one also filled with logs and labrador tea. Above it there is a fine view of Owls Head Mountain. If you miss the point to turn to the pond, but reach a small stream tumbling down the slopes, follow it up to the pond.

The second approach starts from the second rock promontory north of the Carry. Head uphill and to the west to intersect an old road that leads north. The roadway is filled with small spruce; a path is flagged along the roadway. The roadway bends northeast, crosses a stream, and reaches a fork where you angle left away from the roadway. This puts you on the abandoned snowmobile trail that traverses the hillside in a west-north-westerly direction before descending to the outlet. From this point follow the directions as above. This route may be easier walking, but it saves little time because blowdowns and dense growth mean you have to take your time finding the route. Note that the snowmobile trail is incorrectly shown on the new metric USGS Forked Lake map.

Long Lake to the Northway — The Blue Ridge Road

PARTS OF THE Blue Ridge Road are very old, dating to the first route from the Hudson Valley to the northwest. A road from Chester to Canton was authorized in 1812 and went south of Newcomb Lake and through the northwest corner of Hamilton County by way of the south end of Long Lake. In 1826 iron was discovered at Tahawus, compelling a road from Lake Champlain and the Schroon Valley to the mine. In 1828 Judge Duncan McMartin, a State Senator and one of those originally involved in the Tahawus or MacIntyre mine, secured passage of a legislative act calling for the survey of a road from Cedar Point (Port Henry) on Lake Champlain to the western boundary of Essex County. That road crossed the Schroon River north of its confluence with The Branch. That river's name derives from the fact that it is the West Branch of the Schroon.

The Cedar Point Road headed west from the Schroon River toward Clear Pond and continued generally west to the Hudson. It passed near the house of Daniel Tobias Newcomb, some five miles northeast of the present village of Newcomb. The western portion of this road was abandoned about 1849. The present route of the Blue Ridge Road west from Niagara Brook to Newcomb was authorized as the Carthage Road in 1841 and was completed all the way to Jefferson County by 1849. The portion west to Newcomb and the Lower Works of the MacIntyre Mine was apparently completed by 1845.

Almost none of the road from Newcomb to Long Lake is bordered by state lands, but the scenery is not that much different from the turn-of-the-century Forest Commission Report, which noted that the entire fourteen miles of road is "through a magnificent forest." Fortunately, there are two excellent accesses to that forest.

The following outlines mileages to places along the Blue Ridge Road and NY 28N from Northway exit 29 to Long Lake. In the sections describing

126 *Discover the Central Adirondacks*

destinations from these points, mileages to trailheads in the western portion are given starting from Long Lake, and in the eastern portion they are given from the railroad crossing east of the intersection of NY 28 N and the Blue Ridge Road.

Northway - 0
Waterfall on the Branch - 2 miles
Elk Lake Road - 3.7 miles
Hoffman Notch Trailhead - 5 miles
Balancing erratic - 9.8 miles
Boreas River - 11 miles
Picnic overlook - 12.1 miles
Cheney Pond Trail - 12.6 miles
Vanderwhacker Pond - 14.2 miles
Tahawus turn - 17 miles
Railroad crossing - 17.05 miles
Fork to Newcomb or North Creek 28 N - 17.8 miles
(Southern junction NY 28 N - 18.1 miles)
Western junction NY 28 N - 18.25 miles
High Peaks view picnic area - 20 miles
Lake Harris Campground - 21.2 miles
The Hudson River - 21.5 miles
Public Boat Launch - 22.4 miles
Santanoni Preserve - 23.4 miles
Adirondack Visitors Center at Newcomb - 24.4 miles
View of Goodnow over Lodo Pond - 24.9 miles
Huntington Nature trail - 25.05 miles
Goodnow Mountain Trailhead - 26.55 miles
Parking area - picnic spot - 31.8 miles
Northville-Placid Trailhead - 35.7 miles
Long Lake Village, NY 30 - 37.3 miles

55 Long Lake to Tirrell Pond

Northville-Placid Trail segment, hiking, camping
10.2 miles, 5 hours, 1250 feet vertical rise, map IX

This long stretch of the blue-marked Northville-Placid Trail takes you to Tirrell Pond from the north. You will still have to walk 3.25 miles to reach NY 30 north of the Adirondack Museum (see section 41) or 4.6 miles to reach NY 30 opposite the Lake Durant Campground (section 40). Along the trail, there are no views from mountain heights. The forest covering the draw between Burnt and Sabattis mountains is the principal attraction of this route.

A large parking area lies on the south side of NY 28 N, 1.6 miles east of Long Lake Village. The path begins from the eastern side of it, descends into a wetland, crosses a small brook, and continues through the wetland aided by a long boardwalk. The trail is generally south through a damp spruce forest with the boardwalk continuing for the better part of half a mile. You cross a bridge over Sandy Creek at 0.8 mile, a twenty-minute walk from the highway. Just beyond and up a rise, the trail joins a wide, old, well-graded roadway and follows it for 0.4 mile (a ten-minute walk) to intersect the road to the Long Lake Reservoir. The way west leads to private land; you follow the road east on a long level for 0.5 mile to a marked intersection. Note that the roadway continues; the trail makes a turn to the south following another roadway which is gated at the intersection.

You begin a very gentle climb and cross Sandy Creek again, at 2.4 miles, this time without benefit of a bridge, about fifteen minutes from the intersection. A gorge enveloping the stream develops on your left; you cross the stream again; and the gorge now lies on your right. At this point the climb gets a bit stiffer. You can see the outline of Mt. Sabattis through the trees across the gorge to your right. That gorge is now more than 200 feet below the level of trail which hugs the slopes of Burnt Mountain. The trail reaches the town line 0.9 mile from the creek crossing, 3.3 miles into the hike. Just beyond, the trail passes through a poorly drained field and starts to climb again. Maples sheltering the trail thin out as you gain elevation. Strikingly tall paper birch now cover the steep mountainside and shelter an understory of lush ferns. You begin a steep traverse of that hillside to the east to gain the summit ridge. The end of the traverse is almost level, heading north of east across the ridge. An arrow points you to a sharp turn to the left, south, through a small draw to the height-of-land. You can cover the 4.5 miles to this point in just over two hours.

Walk slowly across the height-of-land, savoring the ferns, tall stands of the "fancy fern" as this lacy variety of the evergreen woodfern, *Dryopteris intermedia,* is often called. Unless you really want to make the through trip, you may want to return at this point; the continuing trail is less inviting and rougher walking.

Beyond the height-of-land there is a fairly rapid descent, curving southeast around the head of a draw. The trail grows wider and often wetter. The descent grows less steep and makes a sharp right angle turn 1.3 miles from the height-of-land, a thirty-five-minute walk. The turn leads into a

View of High Peaks from Goodnow

small clearing, with balsam filling the side of the trail and the cover, definitely new growth. A short, covered walk enclosed by spruce and balsam leads to a second, larger marsh, an old beaver flow 6.2 miles from the start. Sundew grow in the sphagnum mats that line the wet area. The walking is bad; you will certainly leave a deep footprint to join the deer hoofprints you are sure to see. Beyond the marsh you climb a small rise, then descend to the level of a small stream that you follow for a short distance before crossing a tributary. The stream flows into a deep gorge that drops away to the right side of the trail. Here the trail changes from its southerly direction to angle southeast up and over and gradually down around the shoulder of a small hill. This section of the trail is very pleasant; the roadway is without ruts and covered with grasses. A small, tumbling creek accompanies it down on the right.

At 7.4 miles, the trail is gated again. Here it reaches private lands and intersects the road to privately owned Salmon Lake. Turn right; and a quarter mile beyond, you reach the bridge over the Salmon River. The walk to this point will have taken nearly four hours so this is a good place to stop for lunch. The trail follows the road east for 0.3 mile through an open field. Watch for the markers pointing the trail back into the woods, a left fork, through a wooded area into another very wet area. Here the split-log base is barely adequate to keep you dry. A sphagnum-lined spruce swamp is no place for a trail! Beyond the 100 feet or so of stringers, the trail heads back into taller forest. The trail here is widely cut, almost a roadway; but as it climbs slightly, the trail narrows. Here it makes a long arc to the east around a hillside and in the next half mile descends to meet another tote road. Arrows point you right on the road, then sharply left along it into a grassy stretch. Markings should keep you from being confused.

The trail continues a gentle descent through a spruce-walled section to yet another marsh. Here the trail is apt to be totally flooded out, but you can manage to cross on a low beaver dam. A hundred feet beyond, the trail turns right in a small open area, then plunges into a spruce thicket again. You make a rock hopping crossing of a small stream and in 150 feet reach the trail junction with the red-marked trail from NY 30, just short of 10 miles from the start. The Tirrell Pond lean-to is 0.3 mile to left, east. The Northville-Placid Trail continues south another 4.6 miles to Lake Durant (section 40).

56 Goodnow Mountain

Marked trail, fire tower, hiking, snowshoeing
3-mile round trip, 2 hours, 1050 feet vertical rise, map X

Goodnow Mountain is a part of the Huntington Forest property owned by SUNY Syracuse School of Environmental Sciences and Forestry. They maintain the trail and keep it open to the public. It is such a pleasant trail to walk, and the view of the High Peaks is so rewarding that you are sure to enjoy it. Since no hunting is allowed on the property, many find this an especially pleasant walk during hunting season in the fall. It is fairly steep but a pretty good trail for a winter snowshoe trip. The trailhead is 10.7 miles east of Long Lake. The school has logged parts of the mountainside, and it definitely is a disturbed area. However, this will not bother you. On the gentle ascent south near the beginning, the trail is enhanced by ditched culverts and well-designed water bars. It arcs through southeast, climbing more steeply, and turns to the east. After half an hour of walking and over half the distance to the summit, the trail crosses a stream. Beyond, a sharp angle to the right takes you past ledges to the foundation of the original fire ranger's cabin. The trail zigzags beneath ledges and reaches a level area. There is a fork at this point, about forty-five minutes into the walk and less than 0.3 mile from the summit. The way left leads to a well house. Shortly beyond on the main trail there is a small, very old horse barn. The continuing route is along a balsam- and spruce-covered ledge, still climbing. You reach an opening in the trees with views south

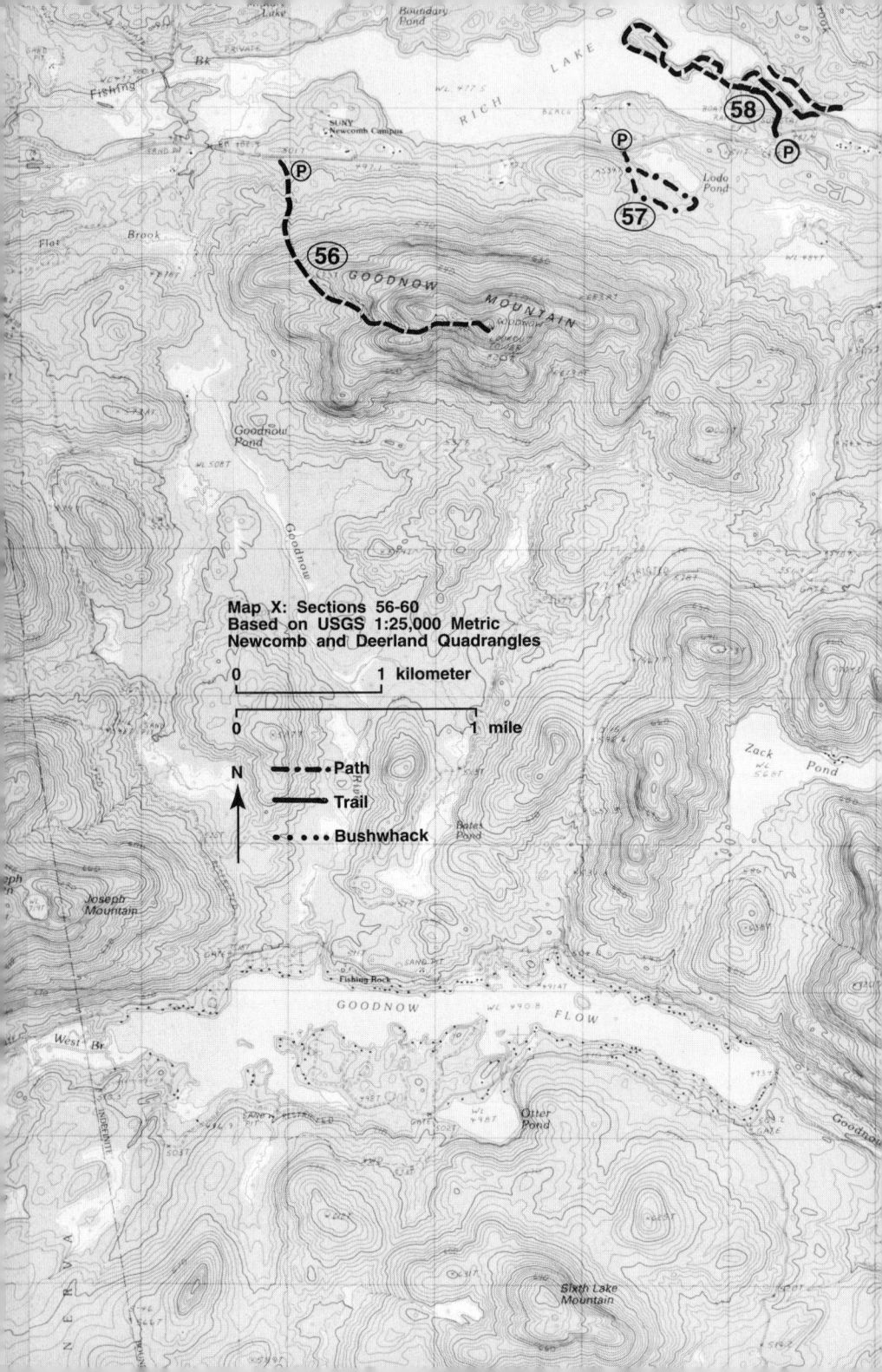

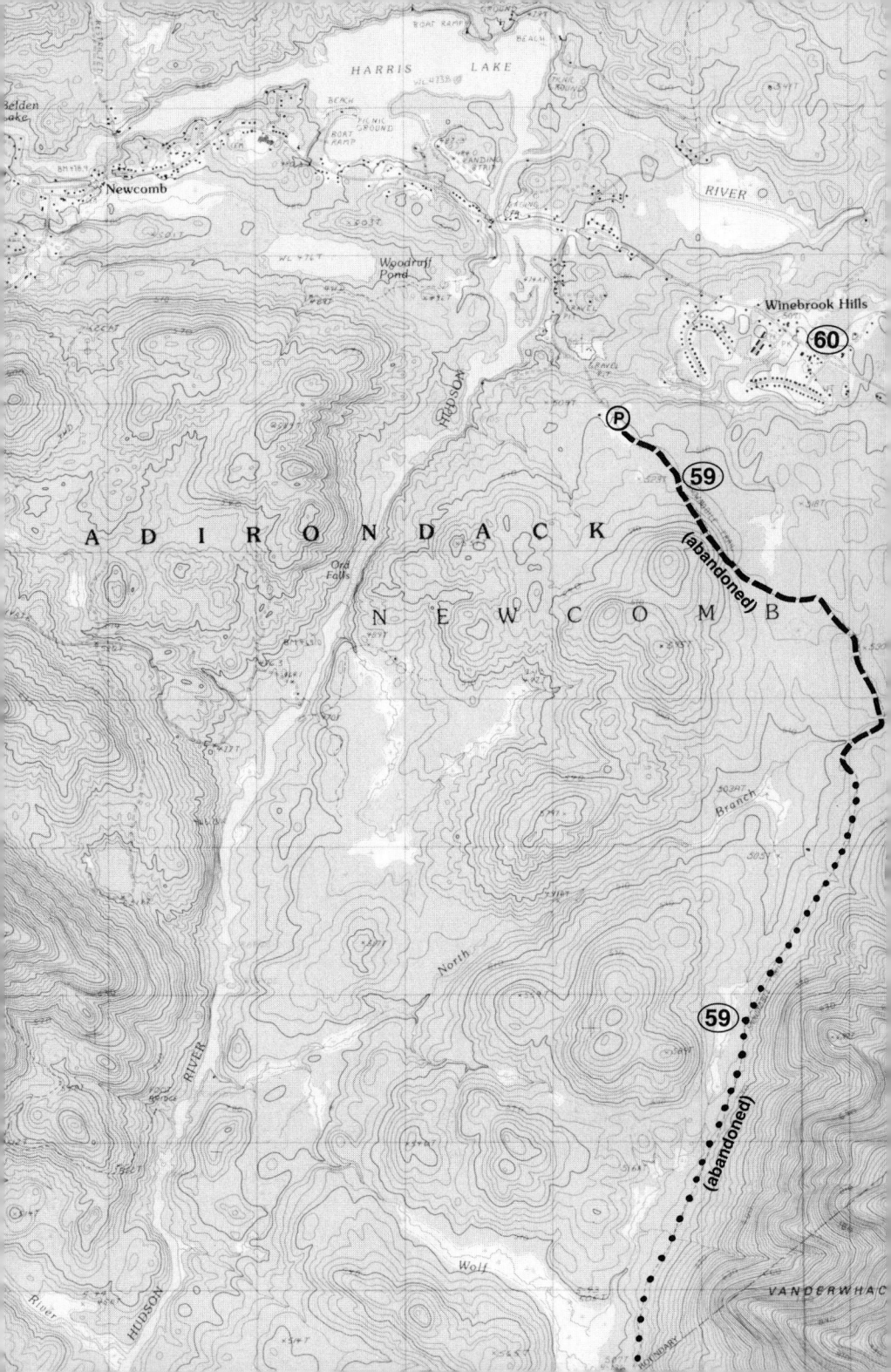

and west with Puffer, Peaked, and Gore mountains clearly outlined on the horizon. A short drop takes you into the col between knobs on the ridge line, a hundred yards below the summit. The tower on the summit is sometimes manned. Even without climbing it you have wonderful views of the High Peaks. You can look down at Rich and Harris lakes. With a map of the High Peaks Wilderness, it is easy to pick out almost all the major peaks to the north.

57 Huntington Forest Nature Trail
0.5 mile, ½ hour, minimal elevation change, map X

This short nature trail is exceptionally well ordered and diverse, except that like many other trails in the Adirondacks, beaver have currently flooded parts of this trail. With a booklet, obtained free of charge from a booth at a parking area on the north side of NY 28 N, 1.5 miles east of the Goodnow Trailhead, you can guide yourself along numbered stops. The half-mile loop starts in a red pine plantation and crosses to the south side of the road. A specimen of every major Adirondack tree species is labeled. The loop passes Lodo Pond, a small bog lake with lots of birds. It continues through a hemlock stand, past a spruce flat, to a hillside covered with northern hardwoods.

58 Adirondack Visitors Interpretive Center at Newcomb
3 miles, relatively level trails, 3 hours, wheelchair-accessible portion, map X

Cedar, hemlock, and pines combine in the typical north-woods forest. The deep, shaded floor of these forests is the most delightful place to walk. Add exquisitely designed trails, boardwalks, and bridges, and weave the trails along the shores of a peninsula jutting out into Rich Lake—and you have the perfect introduction to a north-woods forest. Top this off with views of distant mountains, marshes, and beaver ponds, and you have an experience to treasure. Best of all is the fact that not only are the trails wonderfully groomed so all ages can enjoy them, but one segment is paved for wheelchair access.

The entrance to the Visitors Center is 2.2 miles east of the Goodnow Mountain Trailhead, 1 mile west of the entrance to Santanoni Preserve in Newcomb.

Head north from the Center to the 1.3 mile-long Sucker Brook Trail that winds east along the brook to a bridge. Across the bridge you can turn right to view the remains of the dam, which once enlarged Rich Lake. This trail will ultimately be extended to Santanoni Farm and the complex of trails on Santanoni Preserve. Alternatively, you can turn left to see the beaver dams on Little Sucker Brook and continue into a deep sphagnum wetland. This trail will eventually be extended to a bridge near the outlet of Rich Lake, creating a loop walk.

Heading down the zigzags to the west of the Visitors Center, on the wheelchair-accessible Rich Lake Trail, you cross a boardwalk to an overlook with views of Goodnow Mountain. A bridge leads to the peninsula trail, which has a smooth gravel surface and two overlook spots. Mounds of shells of freshwater clams ring the shore near one resting place.

The Primeval Forest Trail forks from the Rich Lake Trail not far from a giant glacial erratic. It is the steepest of the trails, climbing the bluffs along the shore. You pass a spur to an overlook, then reach a fork in the trail. If you go left you climb some more, descend two staircases, the second of which takes you down beside rock cliffs. Turning now back east, the trail crosses a wide marsh on a long boardwalk, shortly before completing the peninsula loop.

Maps, guideboards, and interpretive signs make it easy to find the routes and discover what is most unusual about the terrain they cross.

59 Wolf Creek
Path and bushwhack, map X

At one time a 9-mile circuit of Vanderwhacker Mountain was designed as a snowmobile trail, combining traditional routes and trails with a newly cut portion. Because of access problems and lack of use, it has been abandoned as a snowmobile trail; and the circuit is virtually impossible, even as a bushwhack. This is most unfortunate because the trail was much enjoyed by cross-country skiers. Portions of it can still be skied though the number of deadfalls make even the easy-to-find areas tedious. Either skiing or hiking from the north to the flow along Wolf Creek remains possible.

Chassins Road heads south from NY 28 N, 0.2 mile east of the bridge over the Hudson. Follow the road to the end and a parking circle in a field. This is private but currently unposted land. The road continues as a trail south of the field. At the first fork, go left. Within 0.5 mile, you reach state land, noticeable by the increasing height of the trees. Corduroy alternates with patches of muck and long, dry stretches. Beautiful stands of tall, very straight yellow birch and maple enrich the walk. Isolated, immense pines and spruce border the roadway.

Just over a mile into the walk, the roadway enters a spruce swamp and crosses a stream. Sphagnum and bunchberry form the understory of the delightful forest that follows. After an hour's walk the roadway reaches an old campsite, where it forks. The way south, left fork, heads downhill and disappears in a large beaver flow. The way right, briefly west, then south, gradually descends into a lush, ferny area that is adjacent to the North Branch of Wolf Creek. Again, the beauty of the deep, rich woods impresses. The path completes its detour of the wet areas by turning left in a spruce forest and climbing ever so slightly above the level of the marsh-filled valley of a tributary of Wolf Creek.

At 2 miles the path now takes a direct course of west of south, following the long, straight valley at the foot of Vanderwhacker Mountain. The valley, like many in the north woods, appears to have two outlet streams, depending on the level of beaver activity. The path generally heads west of south for the next 3 miles, a two-and-a-quarter hour walk. On the way you will cross five streams which flow from draws on the slopes of Vanderwhacker. After the third you will begin to see open marshes to the west. Here the path becomes quite filled with brush and blowdowns that conceal the continuing route. Witch hobble here grows taller than your head, and both witch hobble and maple starts seem to thrive best in the old roadway.

Just beyond the fourth stream crossing, a large beaver flow with open water lies west of the path. It is a nice stopping point. Half a mile beyond it there is another campsite beside the trail. The trash around this one includes, improbably, an old bicycle. The trees surrounding have bear scratches from a good-sized visitor. The road/path appears to end here as it seems pointed at a marsh south of the campsite. Angle left to pick up the path again. There are occasional old snowmobile trail signs.

Just over 0.5 mile farther, the path reaches another stream. Again, the roadway appears to end, and for all but the most adventurous and knowledgeable, the trek should end here as well.

60 High Peaks View Picnic Area
Map X

The Town of Newcomb maintains a roadside picnic area, complete with restrooms, 17.3 miles east of Long Lake, 1.5 miles east of the Hudson Crossing in Newcomb. The view north to the High Peaks is impressive.

61 Vanderwhacker Pond
Unmarked path, camping, fishing, map IV

In the triangle of Wild Forest land north of the Blue Ridge Road, several destinations beckon. The largest accessible pond in the triangle is Vanderwhacker. The beginning of the path is 2.8 miles east of the railroad crossing on the north side of the Blue Ridge Road. All you notice at first is a small cleared area used by campers. The narrow path starts from the west side of it and is marked with a few old blazes though the path is sufficiently well-worn that it is easy enough to follow without markings. The mile-long path climbs 240 feet to the pond and takes a half hour to walk. The scrubby forest near the road soon gives way to taller trees in a nice, open hardwood forest. The path is close to Vanderwhacker Brook, crossing it three times before reaching the pond. Beaver have raised the level of the pond, filling its shores with ghostly skeletons of dead spruce. Birds in profusion perch on them. There is no good path around the pond, but fishermen make their way to a camping spot, a high-and-dry rock ledge, on the northeast corner of the quarter-mile-long pond.

62 Cheney Pond
Short walk, canoeing, picnicking, map IV

Cheney Pond is named for John Cheney, a well-known guide who lived in the Tahawus area. In 1845 Cheney was with David Henderson, an engineer, prospector, and one of the principals in the Tahawus Iron Mine, when Henderson was accidentally killed by a pistol shot while he was camping beside Calamity Brook. Cheney served as guide and hunter for the iron mine; and because of his service to the mine owners he was given a farm site along the Blue Ridge Road.

View across Lester Flow to High Peaks

Cheney himself was shot in the leg at one of the three ponds in the Adirondacks now named for him. From his story, recorded by the writer Charles Lanman, it appears that this pond on the south side of the Blue Ridge Road is probably the one where Cheney's accident occurred. (Headley and Donaldson give the pond as the one a mile west of Lake Sanford: but Lanman, quoting Cheney, gives the distance as fourteen miles from his MacIntyre [Tahawus] home. Regardless of whether or not this is the right pond, it is a good story.)

Lanman traveled about the United States and Canada, fishing and hunting and writing his exploits for a public newly awakened to his *Adventures in the Wilds*. He spent several days in the company of John Cheney, climbing Mt. Marcy with him and recording the tales of Cheney's dogs and exploits. Quoting Cheney, he wrote:

> I never was so badly hurt in hunting any animal as I have been in hunting deer. It was while chasing a buck on Cheney's Lake (which was named after me by Mr. Henderson in commemoration of my escape) that I once shot myself in a very bad way. I was in a canoe, and had laid my pistol down by my side, when, as I was pressing hard upon the animal, my pistol slipped under me in some queer way, and went off, sending a ball into my leg, just above the ankle, which came out just below the knee. I knew something terrible had happened, and though I thought that I might die, I was determined that the deer should die first; and I did succeed in killing him before he reached the shore. But, soon as the excitement was over, the pain I felt before was increased a thousand-fold, and I felt as if all the devils in hell were dragging at my leg, the weight and the agony were so great. I had never suffered so before,

and I thought it strange. You may not believe it, but when that accident happened, I was fourteen miles from home, and yet, even with that used-up leg, I succeeded in reaching my home, where I was confined to my bed from October until April. That was a great winter for hunting which I missed; but my leg got entirely well, and is now as good as ever.

The dirt road which leads to Cheney Pond is a right turn from the Blue Ridge Road, 4.3 miles east of the railroad crossing on NY 28 N. A trailhead sign indicates 11 miles to Irishtown on a snowmobile and hiking trail, via Cheney Pond, Lester Dam, and Minerva Stream.

Vehicles do use the road which is quite rutted and often washed out. Since no maintenance is done on it, four-wheel-drive vehicles are a minimum. Unless you are carrying a canoe, this ten-minute walk should not tempt you to drive. Even with a canoe, it is only 0.5 mile to the pond, and a wheeled cart would be ideal here for those who cannot carry any distance.

The road forks at 0.4 mile—just after a muddy spot which could stop most vehicles. Cheney Pond is to the left. The entire route to the pond is downhill, a 170-foot descent. There is a campsite with a fire ring and outhouse at the end of the roadway and an easy place to launch your canoe.

The pond is not so big as it was when it was enlarged by the flooding caused by the Lester Flow Dam on the Boreas. There are numerous campsites around the pond and a handsome sand beach on the far eastern shore—good place for children to swim. Ducks nest in the quiet corners of the pond, and fishermen regularly visit it, so it must be productive—though no reports confirm this.

63 Lester Flow on Foot
Marked trail, hiking, snowmobile trail, skiing, picnicking
2.6 miles, 1 hour, minimal elevation change, map IV

The right fork of the trail to Cheney Pond, above, leads south to Lester Dam in 2.2 miles along a fairly easy and uneventful trail. You cross a barrier to vehicles and see markers for the Forest Preserve 100 yards from the fork. The road leads up a slight grade, then down to pass below a beaver dam on a small stream. The dam leaks water into the trail. The rest of the trail is level and direct.

Depending on water level, you can cross the Boreas on the slippery logs remaining from the last dam, which raised the water in the flow 10 to 15

The remains of Lester Dam

feet above its present level. In moderate water, you can find rocks to improvise a crossing downstream from the dam site. In high water, do not try to cross. In winter, with good ice, you can cross above the dam on the frozen flow.

If you are able to cross to the far side, walk along the paths upriver on the Boreas. Huge piles of shells from freshwater clams are imbedded in the sandy wash of this glacial basin. Look 200 feet upriver for a rock ledge embedded with a bolt and ring, which held booms to keep logs from the dam. Most of all, you will enjoy the distant panorama of the High Peaks across the flow. It is a wonderful view that includes Marcy, Haystack, Basin Saddleback, Gothics, the Range, and Sawteeth. In the foreground to the right are Wolf Pond Mountain with Boreas Mountain behind.

A large rock shelf above the dam site is a good place for a picnic and for contemplating the dam's history. The first dam was built in the late 1800s by Finch Pruyn & Co. A second dam of rock and stone with log cribbing was built in 1931 under the supervision of John "Jack" Donohue, who was the agent for the company in the area and who lived in North River. The plans for the dam show the upstream top was to be 320 feet across, and it was over 30 feet high. The thickness of 30 to 40 feet can still be seen in the foundation remains in the streambed.

It must have been an impressive sight when the water was released in the spring to provide a surge to float pulp wood down the Boreas and into the Hudson. The dam was last used in 1951. It was breached shortly after, and the last three or four feet washed completely away about 1980, returning the Boreas to its previous size and level.

64 Lester Flow by Canoe
Canoeing, picnicking, exploring, fishing, map IV

If you carry a canoe to Cheney Pond, you can enjoy a fairly level canoe trip that is over 6 miles round trip. Note, however, that even though this is almost flat water, the river's current can be strong, depending on the height of the Boreas. Cross Cheney Pond and look for the shallow outlet into the Boreas in the northeast corner, almost hidden by sand dunes. You can paddle and push your canoe down the outlet for 200 yards before it becomes too narrow. You will have to carry or line the last 150 feet to the Boreas, which, at this point, is 30 feet wide and only a foot or two deep in low summer water. You can paddle upstream past several bends to the rapids.

Downstream the river meanders its serpentine way for two miles along what was the keel of the flow. It is an easy trip, requiring only minimal maneuvering around several turns to avoid hitting rocks. The current hardly seems to sweep you along; you will not feel it until you notice the exertion required to head back upstream. Halfway downstream to the dam, there is a large rock outcrop on the east side for a picnic and a panoramic view of the mountains to the north. It takes about an hour of paddling before the two pine-covered shores appear to meet, and you hear the roar of water where the dam once stood. The rock ledge protruding east of the dam site is a good place to stop and rest. The pool is deep enough to fish. It is a beautiful place with river noises, the wide marsh, and the impressive view of the High Peaks to the north.

It takes at least an hour and a half to paddle back up the Boreas and across Cheney Pond so allow four or more hours for this trip and a picnic, longer if you plan to fish the pond and river.

65 Blue Ridge Road to Irishtown
Marked snowmobile trail, hiking, skiing
11.5 miles, 6 hours, 670-foot descent, maps III, IV

To make this through trip, quite a bit of time is needed to jockey cars into position at either end of this trail because of the distance to drive between trailheads. It is worth the effort since this is a great one-day hike with many things to see along the way. To park one car in the south, drive north on county route 24 from Olmstedville. This becomes Carl Hill Road (Hoffman Road on the USGS map) as it curves east, heading for Schroon Lake. You pass Irishtown, the second left fork. Take the next left turn, 1.3 miles from Irishtown, and continue bearing right for 0.6 mile to a parking turnout. Driving farther north is not practical. Use a good road map to find your way west from Irishtown to Minerva for the trip north on 28 N and east on the Blue Ridge Road to the northern trailhead, the same as for Cheney Pond, where a DEC guideboard indicates "Irishtown 11 miles." Start from the north, heading as you would for Cheney Pond (section 62), not just because this makes the trip downhill, but because if you cannot cross the Boreas, you have only 2.6 miles to return to your car.

Walk to Lester Dam and cross the Boreas (section 63). After crossing the Boreas at 2.6 miles, walk briefly upstream and inland, over moss- and lichen-covered rocks that cling to the shallow soil. Within 100 yards you spot a snowmobile trail marker. The trail is generally heading northeast, paralleling the flow, but way back from it. Numerous blowdowns obscure the trail, occasionally making it hard to discern.

After a twenty-minute walk past the dam, short of a mile, the trail makes a turn to the east. Here you see the first of the Wilderness Area boundary signs. The Hoffman Notch Wilderness Area lies to the east, and this snowmobile trail is its western boundary.

After another ten minutes or so, the trail curves southeast, a course it will hold until you cross an eastern tributary of Minerva Stream. You shortly cross the headwaters of a western tributary of Minerva Stream, and continue level, then gently downhill. The woods and the condition of the trail both improve. You reach and cross a northern tributary of Minerva Stream without the aid of the washed-out snowmobile bridge. This spot is 2.4 miles from Lester Dam, an hour-and-a-quarter walking time and 5 miles from the start.

James C. Dawson near Lester Dam. Ring was used to boom logs.

The trail continues southeast, the trees becoming taller all the time with red spruce, cedar, and tall pine sheltering the trail. The old road origins of the trail become more and more evident, but this brings an increase in the number of wet places, which are usually associated with level roadways. The trail skirts southwest of a sphagnum and spruce swamp and continues on to an alder swamp. Here, at 6 miles, you cross the eastern tributary of Minerva Stream, the one that has plunged steeply from Bailey Hill. It is a mile, thirty minutes, between the tributaries.

The trail now takes a southerly direction, briefly following the stream, with steep mountain slopes to the east. Watch for the large pyramidal glacial erratic like a small cottage thatched in polypodies. Behind the erratic, there is a small waterfall where the stream tumbles over flat rock slabs. Just beyond this, the trail crosses to the west side of the stream; the double cable here at 6.2 miles could assist you if the water is high. The trail stays close to the stream with its tiny waterfalls for a short while, then pulls away.

Nearly a mile south of the Bailey Hill tributary crossing, another half-hour walk, you reach a large meadow with tiny Mud Pond invisible behind the brushy borders. The view across it is to an unnamed mountain with exposed cliffs. A large beaver dam has flooded the trail, and a new red-flagged route has been cut through a spruce thicket to circle around it. At the outlet of Mud Pond there is a large log bridge. Five minutes later, at 7.4 miles, you reach a private inholding. The last part of the trail follows the access road to these inholdings. The trail/roadway fords the stream, then climbs to higher ground. Unfortunately, it remains well above stream level for the next 2.6 miles. You can often hear it roaring below, telling of intriguing rapids and falls in the gorge below; for, with the addition of Hewitt Pond Brook, Minerva Stream has become quite large. The hemlock woods which cling to the steep slopes of Hayes Mountain make a lovely setting for the trail. The route is gradually, steadily, downhill.

An hour suffices for the walk from the inholding to a crossing of another of Minerva Stream's tributaries at 10 miles, this one coming from a deep draw between Hayes Mountain and Cobble Hill. You pass a beaver meadow over which you can see Green Mountain to the west. A large clearing 0.9 mile from the tributary has a house overlooking the stream. Other cabins follow, and in 0.6 mile you reach your car. The sign may have said 11 miles to Irishtown, but it scales out at 11.5 miles to the parking spot short of Irishtown, a long walk if it were not for the fact that so much of it was over one of the Adirondack's better old hiking roads.

66 Cheney Pond Overlook
Picnic site, map IV

A dirt road, 4.9 miles east of the railroad crossing, just 0.5 mile east of the Cheney Pond Trailhead, leads south from the Blue Ridge Road to a lovely cleared picnic site. The view is across the valley of the Boreas toward Lester Flow with Texas Ridge to the east. Cheney Pond is directly south. Vanderwhacker Mountain dominates the western horizon.

This is a must-visit spot at which to become acquainted with the northern portion of the region covered by this guide. Combine it with a short walk to Cheney Pond or the walk along the Boreas.

67 Boreas Explorations
Paths and bushwhacks to quiet spots, map IV

Paths of sorts, combined with a bit of bushwhacking, provide the basis for exploring the Boreas River from the Blue Ridge Road. The bridge is almost 6 miles east of the railroad crossing. On the north side of the road and east of the river, there is a large parking turnout, a picnic area beside the river, and an outhouse. It is a quiet place, and you often see travelers pausing there.

On the south side of the road, two paths follow the banks of the river; and in low water, you can cross downstream and use them to make a loop walk.

The path on the east is the better-worn route. It starts from the end of a parking turnout and looks almost as if it should be the beginning of a roadway. The path plunges into a cedar swamp with several concealed campsites. Part of the way the path is close to the river, and at one point it almost touches a giant boulder that extends out into the stream. Another boulder rests midstream above a quiet pool.

Imagine the year is 1844, and you are watching Charles Lanman. He wrote of his trip which started from Lyndsey's Tavern on the Schroon.

> Our first day's tramp took us about fifteen miles, through a hilly, thickly wooded, and houseless wilderness, to the Boreas River, where we found a ruined log shantee, in which we concluded to spend the night. We reached this lonely spot at about three o'clock in the afternoon; and having previously been told that the Boreas was famous for trout, two of us started after a mess of fish, while the fiddler was appointed to the office of wood-chopper to the expedition. The Boreas at this point is about one hundred feet broad,—winds

Brace Dam

through a woody valley, and is cold, rapid, and clear. The entire river does not differ materially, as I understand, from the point alluded to, for its waters an unknown wilderness. I bribed my farmer friend to ascend the river, and having picked a variety of flies, I started down the stream. I proceeded nearly half a mile, when I came to a still water pool, which seemed to be quite extensive, and very deep. At the head of it, midway in the stream, was an immense boulder, which I succeeded in surmounting, and whence I threw a red hackle for upwards of three hours. I never saw trout jump more beautifully, and it was my rare luck to basket thirty-four; twenty-one of which averaged three-quarters of a pound, and the remaining thirteen were two-pounders.

The path along the Boreas to the confluence with Durgin Brook is less than half a mile long. It continues as a fishermen's route along Durgin Brook, gradually disappearing.

On the west side of the Boreas, a path leads to picnic sites and one particularly handsome camping spot on a balsam-covered knoll. After passing the midstream boulder, the trail gradually disappears in the tall grasses of the meadow beside the stillwater. Blackberries are filling the meadow. Bushwhack through the meadow to the cascade below the rapids. Below the cascade you can find pieces of chains and other abandoned logging equipment.

Long Lake to the Northway   145

If the water level permits, you can cross the river at the head of the cascade and make your way up the east bank, first through a disturbed patch of lichens and blueberries, then through the tall grasses to Durgin Brook. Here you will have to search for logs or rocks to improvise a crossing. While hints of old roadways are everywhere, no continuous route seems to exist today.

68 Brace Dam
Path, camping, fishing, map IV

The beginning of the road on the west side of the Boreas, which leads to Brace Dam, is on private land. The road is marked private, and vehicular traffic is not allowed. Sportsmen walk the road or go along a short section of the banks of the Boreas to reach the place the road enters state land. The roadway leads 1.5 miles north from the Blue Ridge Road to the site of another logging dam. Those who had worked for Finch Pruyn & Co. believe it was used with the dam at Lester Flow to flood logs from the foothills of the High Peaks.

The roadway reaches a gravel pit in 400 yards, and state land is shortly beyond. Only a small part of the distance is the trail within sight of the river, but one section is quite close to a handsome stillwater. Old roads can be fun to walk, and this is no exception. Needles from balsam and spruce cushion the trail. You can walk to the dam site in just over half an hour. There is a camping spot just west of the dam site and another 200 yards north. A small rapids lies just below the dam of which only protruding log stringers remain.

Besides being a quiet destination reached by a short walk, the stillwater above deserves to be explored by canoe. From the dam site, the view over the flow is toward North River Mountains and Cheney Cobble.

69 Balancing Rock
Map IV

Look to the north side of the Blue Ridge Road, 1.2 miles east of the Boreas. There is a curiosity here which deserves a moment's pause: A picture appears in Miller's 1919 *Geology of the Schroon Lake Quadrangle* with the caption:

A rounded glacial boulder of Marcy anorthosite fully 14 feet in diameter resting in a remarkably balanced position upon another boulder of the same kind of rock by the Blue Ridge-Boreas River Road.
The author notes that the lower boulder
is partially buried in glacial drift...Both are notably rounded, suggesting transportation for a number of miles at least...It scarcely seems possible that the upper boulder can retain such a position and yet it remains there in spite of an attempt some years ago to pry it off.

70 Hoffman Notch

Marked trail, hiking, skiing, snowshoeing
3.6 miles one way to Big Marsh, 2½ hours, 550 feet vertical rise; 7.6 miles to Loch Muller, 6 hours, 550 feet vertical rise, maps I, XI

After more than a decade the beaver have been thwarted, or at least their efforts no longer impede those who wish to enjoy the north entrance to the Hoffman Notch Trail. The trail leads into one of the loveliest mountain passes, through mature forests, beside streams and wetlands, all the way to the trailhead at Loch Muller (section 7). Beaver had flooded the low lands between The Branch and the confluence of Sand Pond and Hoffman Notch brooks. A new footbridge and a rerouted trail allow you to circle the once-flooded lands and almost stay dry while doing it. If beaver rebuild their dams, and they surely will, the beginning of the trail may be flooded again; so if you are planning to walk this route through from the south, you ought to check out the beginning of the trail on the north first so you do not have to make an unnecessarily wet crossing.

The northern mile of trail crosses private lands. It begins to the west of The Branch and heads downhill on a dirt road to stream level. It then traverses a lovely cedar stand where both sides of the trail are posted against camping. The trail crosses the joined brooks on the big new hikers bridge and then circles way east and south to avoid the beaver flows though the marked route may not completely avoid flooded marshes here. Next, the trail crosses a small stream on a slippery log, definitely a challenge, and heads back west along the stream and the marshes beside it. Finally, the trail climbs southwesterly through the edge of the forest to a power line. The trail continues southwest diagonally across the fields below the power line and, finally, after a mile, rejoins the old roadway that was the route of the traditional trail.

(Note that if you are walking north, several places in the rerouted trail may be hard to find. The first is at the meadow under the power line. Head east under the power line for 100 yards to find the place the trail enters the woods. After angling east along slopes, the trail takes a left fork where a more obvious skid road heads uphill and straight ahead. The last impediment is the meadow beside the brook where tall weeds conceal the route where it is continuing east, against logic.)

South of the power lines, the trail is along the old roadway. It is well marked and easy to follow. A quarter mile past the power line, the trail enters Forest Preserve land. It then climbs and at 1.4 miles reaches a ford crossing of Hoffman Notch Brook. In winter this can be a difficult place to cross. An old trail shown on the 1953 series USGS as continuing on the eastern side of the brook is completely overgrown.

The trail on the west keeps following a roadway, which leads past the ruins of an ancient tractor. The next 1.2 miles of trail are exceptionally handsome. In it the trail climbs 400 feet through the narrow draw between Hornet Cobbles and Washburn Ridge. Dense hemlock groves shelter the Notch Brook as it tumbles through numerous small cascades. Huge boulders, some as large as houses, choke the valley. Near the head of this deep draw, cliffs range across the face of Washburn Ridge. In wet weather you can spot several small chutes of water plunging 50 or more feet from the cliff tops. They freeze into colorful columns in winter, stained in shades of brown, blue, and green. In summer, watch out for the poison ivy growing on the slopes below the cliffs, but do detour from the trail to inspect the cliffs.

If you are skiing, note that this section has some very narrow and steep places that require some skill. Traveling north here is for experienced skiers only.

At 2.4 miles, there must have been an old logging camp. The remains of a cookstove made at the Rochester Co-op Foundry in the 1860s or 1870s marks the spot. Just beyond, the trail crosses to the east side of the brook. Both this and the next crossing are without benefit of a bridge; and, if the water is too high, you are advised to bushwhack along the west bank for another quarter mile, thus avoiding both crossings. If you choose not to cross the brook, bushwhack along the western shore to the bend in the Hoffman Notch Brook. Here you only have to cross the tiny stream that drains the north slopes of the Notch to intersect the trail at the point where it heads southwest toward Big Marsh and away from the brook.

If you do cross, the trail follows the east bank to the point the brook angles southeast. The trail to the Notch crosses the brook for the second time here at 2.7 miles. The brook flows from two sources, one from a draw

Views from Boreas Mountain

high in the Blue Ridge Range between Texas Ridge and Hornet Cobbles. The other drains a tiny pond in Hornet Notch, just over half a mile from the head of the draw. Old maps show a trail following that source to the pond, but no trace of it can be found.

You may have to work to find the continuing route without getting wet. Beyond this point the trail winds west of south, then south, on a relatively level course, close to the eastern slopes of Washburn Ridge. The trail is becoming overgrown and filled with nettles, and many of the small bridges are almost gone. It continues through the high valley which opens out 0.9 mile from the crossing to the pond called Big Marsh, 3.6 miles from the Blue Ridge Road. For the continuing trail to Loch Muller see section 7.

71 Boreas Mountain

Trail, hiking, snowshoeing
3.4 miles one way, 2½ hour climb, 2050-foot (641 meters) ascent from The Branch crossing, red markings, map XI

One mountain north of the Blue Ridge Road has been included in this Central guide: Boreas. It is almost a High Peak, but at 3683 feet (1151 meters) it is not quite; it belongs to that group, which includes Goodnow and Vanderwhacker, that offers spectacular views of the High Peaks from the south. And, of that group, Boreas is undoubtedly the best.

Drive 3.2 miles north on the Elk Lake Road to a parking turnout on the left. (No winter parking here, though.) The trail starts steeply down through a second growth forest; forests are this route's only drawback. The trail traverses private land all the way, and most of the land has been logged in recent times and will undoubtedly be logged again. Signs warn against hunting, fishing, trapping, or trespassing away from the trail. The trail approaches a road that comes in on the right, then veers left away from it to cross a log bridge over The Branch at 0.4 mile. The trail, now a narrow footpath, is slightly grown. The route is west or slightly north of west. In less than twenty minutes, at 0.7 mile, you cross the outlet of a beaver marsh beside a large beaver dam. You circle the flooded area, glimpse Boreas ahead over the marsh, then in a couple minutes detour right where the trail used to go straight ahead. This detour takes you well away from the flooded area on a long circuit that ends at nearly 1 mile with a rock-hop crossing of a stream that feeds the marsh. Shortly you cross a small field, heading diagonally across to the right.

The trail follows the stream, then heads sharply left, away from the stream bed and up to intersect another logging road. (On the return, a sign marked Trail alerts you to leave the roadway and plunge down the slope to stream level.) The trail briefly follows this road, then crosses the stream and continues on a ridge above the stream. After a rock-hop crossing of a stream at 1.6 miles, the road angles right, but the trail goes left and down to cross the stream again on an old bridge. Still following the stream, which is on the right now, you begin to climb. The trail crosses a tributary stream and continues along a severely eroded old logging road.

150

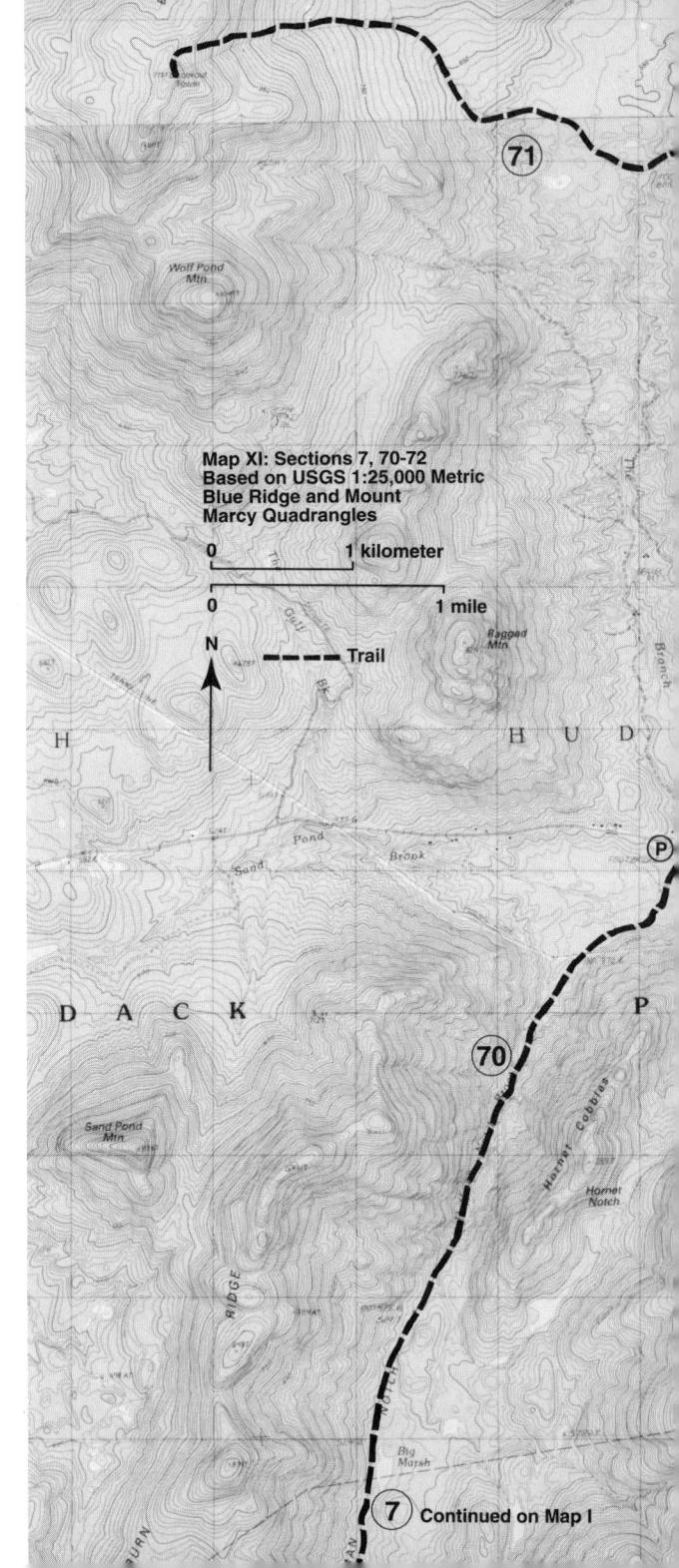

151

Past a small clearing, there is a V in the roadway; the trail takes the right fork. A short uphill leads to a field at 2.4 miles and the old site of the fire observer's cabin. You have just under a mile left to the summit but 1150 feet left to climb.

You cross a small stream at the edge of the meadow and immediately begin the steep climb. The stream you had been following is still there on your left, out of sight. The way is steep; you cross a very small stream; then within twenty minutes from the clearing, the forest changes to spruce, balsam, and paper birch. Water flows down the trail, and the way continues very steeply.

The trail angles left, almost southwest along the narrow ridge line, zigzagging steeply toward the summit knob. The way is steeper and steeper; the forest is marked by dying spruce. An hour and a quarter from the cabin site, watch for a sharp left turn to the summit knob. Then, in less than a hundred yards, the trail forks. Flags direct you right to a lookout to the west and southwest with Santanoni the obvious distant feature. The way right leads to the summit with the foundation of the old fire tower. Fortunately, there has been some clearing on the summit, for the view northeast is less obstructed than previously. The view encompasses the Dixes, Macomb and Hough across Elk Lake, Sunrise to its east, and Camelhump, Niagara, (little) Nippletop and Owl Pate.

Walk left to a small rock outcrop that explodes into the High Peaks panorama from Skylight on the west, with Marcy behind, Panther Gorge, Haystack, Basin, Saddleback, Gothics, Armstrong on the horizon, Pinnacle, Blake and Colvin, in front, leading up to Nippletop. Over Hunters Pass, and between Nippletop and Dix, you see Giant.

It takes less than forty minutes to return to the cabin site, an hour more (about the same as on the ascent) to return to your car.

72 Waterfall on The Branch

From the Hoffman Notch Trailhead all the way east to the Northway, both sides of the Blue Ridge Road are privately owned. This fact plus the barrier presented by The Branch preclude any northern access to the Blue Ridge Mountains and Hoffman Mountain. At the community of Blue Ridge you will find commercial accommodations. This is near an especially lovely waterfall on The Branch, 3 miles east of the Hoffman Trailhead, 2 miles west of the Northway. Whatever the season, it is always pleasant to stop for a look at the falls from roadside.

North River to Indian Lake

THE RECTANGLE NORTH of NY 28, extending from North Creek to Indian Lake, and south of the Hudson, contains the heart of the central Adirondack region. It comprises the famed Blue Ledge and the deep Hudson River Gorge and more than a dozen ponds which vary from tiny bogs to mile-long bodies of water. The outlet of OK Slip Pond forms the fabled falls, reportedly the tallest in the park, before reaching the Hudson.

While the majority of the land is state owned, almost all of the roadside along NY 28 is privately owned. The pattern of ownership manages to block access to most of the ponds or at least make it very difficult. At present, the Blue Ledge, OK Slip Falls, and the confluence of the Indian and the Hudson are all inaccessible.

Because of access problems, this chapter contains only a few expeditions in a region which should have a dozen or more. The area contains no state trails. Hopefully, state plans to acquire parts of this area will be completed before too long. Then the Hudson Gorge Primitive Area will become consolidated into one of the Adirondacks' most wonderful wilderness areas. If the Finch Pruyn property is acquired, the public will be able to walk the road and head from it to Casey Mountain, OK Slip Pond and Falls, the Blue Ledge, and Carter ponds, using a fairly well-developed network of logging roads and foot trails.

This chapter has been taken out of logical order and placed at the end of the guide, anticipating a revised edition with numerous additions, as soon as the acquisitions are completed.

73 Along the Hudson River—The Greyhound Bus Stop

2 miles one way, 1 hour, following old railroad tracks, map II

Most of the new routes that will eventually be open in the Hudson Gorge Primitive Area are those that once were used by river drivers—that wild breed of men who struggled to keep logs floating down the Hudson and its tributaries to mills near Glens Falls. Traditionally, logs were rafted down more placid rivers. The rocky and often violent Adirondack rivers inspired a new invention, the floating of single logs, a practice which was introduced into the Adirondacks in 1813.

The logs were boomed up at Glens Falls, and records show that the annual log drives increased until 1872 when over a million logs containing 200 million board feet were floated down the Hudson. In those days the logger did not cut the bottom foot of stump, and he cut nothing under 19" in diameter. But so large were the trees that often one tree yielded two or three standard logs, 13 feet long.

These huge logs often choked the Hudson River, creating immense jams that the river drivers worked to free. Log drivers knew the Hudson River gorge as a nightmare of danger that would test their skill and perhaps take their lives. On log drives that started at Newcomb, the drivers smoked their pipes and relaxed and even rode the logs through the flat river stretches. But, when the drive passed the mouth of the Cedar River and approached the Indian River, there was always a dull roar from the gorge. Drivers knew that they had tough times ahead.

Known as the "jam stretch," the Gorge was full of narrows, ledges, huge boulders, whirlpools, and eddies. Drivers faced death every day as they attempted to break up the jams. Out on a jam, a huge log had to be released with a pike pole or perhaps from a boat floating below the jam. When all else failed, the jam was dynamited.

As early as the 1850s, the state legislature passed laws which made Adirondack rivers "public highways for floating logs." The mass of logs carried by the spring floods and releases from many dams caused great damage to river narrows. Ledges were blasted to widen them and prevent jams.

River drivers were paid $2.00 a day to face these hardships, wearing woolen clothing that was often wet all day. At night they returned to open-faced lean-tos, some of them 40 feet wide with their back to the river and four open fires in front. Camps were near the mouth of Carter Brook,

Giant cedars and hemlocks at Whortleberry Pond

OK Slip Brook, and Baker Brook, just above Harris Rift.

A trip through the river by raft or canoe is the best way to sample the gorge, but you can ski or walk along the D & H Railroad right of way from North River to the Greyhound Bus Stop, the last of the narrow rapids. No trains currently use the tracks.

This is a scenic trip with open hardwoods on each side of the track. The river is on the east side of the railroad and, after the first half mile, you are close enough to see the river and hear its roar. The best time to take this hike is in the late spring when the river is high and whitewater canoeists, kayakers, and rafters are running it.

Drive west out of North River toward Indian Lake. In less than 0.5 mile from Thirteenth Lake Road, NY 28 crosses the railroad track. There is a road to the right, north, 200 yards beyond the tracks. Park along NY 28 and walk north beside the tracks. You will see a large industrial building on the right which is the processing plant and offices of Barton Mines. Some of the men at the plant feed deer in winter so you may see some whitetails as you pass behind the building.

156 *Discover the Central Adirondacks*

You cross Raquette Brook in 0.6 mile, then draw closer to the Hudson. After 1.6 miles, you cross Griffin Brook; and soon after that, you will see a large rock protruding into the river, just below the tracks. It marks a rock ledge which lies diagonally underwater, setting up a drop with large, uneven hydraulic force. This is the place to eat lunch and watch action on the river.

Occasionally, here at the Greyhound Bus Stop, probably named for the rock that is as big as a bus, you will see canoes flip or rafters bounced out of their rafts as the hydraulic creates a mean "stopper" wave. It is easy to get good pictures of boats and rafts as you are so close to the action.

A short distance upriver, on the west side of the tracks, there is a pipe with running water coming from a spring—a remnant of the logging days on the river. If you keep walking a total of three miles from NY 28, you will come to the bridge over the Hudson near the mouth of the Boreas River (section 29). There are no hiking trails leading from this point so you must return along the tracks.

74 Ross, Whortleberry and Big Bad Luck Ponds

Hiking, camping, cross-country skiing, snowshoeing, map V

Only two of the ponds—Ross and Whortleberry—north of NY 28 can be reached by path or trail. With a short bushwhack you can reach Big Bad Luck Pond, the largest in this Primitive Area. Hunters and campers keep this route fairly clear of deadfalls so it is an excellent route for cross-country skiing.

The route to Ross Pond is unmarked and begins 6 miles east of the Abanakee Bridge and just east of a new house and pond built at the former beginning of this route. There are no signs and no easy parking here along the highway. A narrow path heads downslope on the north side of the road through state land that touches NY 28. It is wet walking beside the dam of the new pond, which is posted. In two minutes this path intersects the old roadway and turns to follow it. (On the return, a big—8" diameter—yellow bullet marks the place you have to leave the roadway.)

The path along the old road starts gently downhill through a nice rich forest, heading generally north. Beside a hemlock knoll there is an old foundation. (From here you could bushwhack east to the cliffs on Casey

Mountain. It is a steep bushwhack to the cliffs for views over the Siamese Ponds Wilderness, but the approach is all on state land. An easier approach from the east uses roads to the old garnet mine on Casey, but that starts on private lands so is not yet a possibility.)

On the path, you cross several small brooks, then after twenty minutes (about one mile) you see a marshy area on the left created by Bell Mountain Brook. Here the path swings northeast to parallel the brook. Ten minutes later, not quite half a mile, you cross Bell Mountain Brook on the remains of an old bridge. The path has narrowed as it climbs northwesterly, up through a draw. For skiers this stretch may be hard to navigate on the return. In another fifteen minutes, as you approach the height-of-land in the draw, watch for green paint on a rock.

If you are headed for Whortleberry or Big Bad Luck ponds, stay straight ahead to reach the height-of-land at 2000 feet and after less than 2 miles and an hour from the highway. From this point it is 0.75 mile down a gradual slope to Ross Pond, which lies at 1750 feet.

Ross Pond is not boggy, but neither is it very deep, twenty feet at most. It is a pretty pond with a small island and a wooded shoreline of spruce, balsam, and beech, and a few alders and shrubs. Beavers repeatedly dam the outlet with the result that you can find outlets in two different locations. A large rock on the east side is a good place to fish with the possibility of a campsite nearby.

A path goes around the west side of Ross Pond and then heads north, still following the old road to Whortleberry Pond. From Ross to Whortleberry is an easy path of about 0.75 mile that goes up a slight rise and then drops to the pond elevation of 1670 feet. As you go north, Pine Mountain appears across the wide valley to the northwest; the pond lies at the foot of the eastern slopes of that mountain. As you approach the pond, you cross an open area with bare rock outcrops and pines filling niches pioneered by lichens. If you continue straight north here, you reach the pond in the vicinity of some unusual ledges, which parallel the shore of the pond. Impressive pines line the shore.

If you head right, the path takes you to an intersection where a blue blaze marks the trail right to private lands. The church camp to the east maintains the paths, explaining why they are so easy to follow. (You can walk east, right along an esker, viewing the marshes beside the outlet of Whortleberry Pond for a quarter of a mile before you reach private land.) Turn left at the intersection and in 150 feet reach and cross the outlet and walk the north shore west for 100 yards to a lovely campsite beside the water. Because Forest Preserve land ends about halfway between Whortle-

berry and OK Slip ponds, it is not possible to go from Whortleberry to the Hudson River Gorge without permission.

If you are headed first for Ross Pond, it is preferable to turn right at the green-marked rock. This narrow path winds gently downhill and northeast through an impressively tall forest of white ash, birch, maple, and beech with hemlock patches. In fifteen minutes, a little over 0.5 mile, you drop to the hemlock-sheltered rock ledge on the east side of the pond. From here you can bushwhack along the eastern shore, first passing a red-flagged path that leads northeast to the church camp. Continue around the north side of the pond and over a ridge to intersect the path along the old roadway.

Big Bad Luck Pond lies west of Ross Pond and is entirely in Forest Preserve land. It is possible to hike from Ross Pond to Big Bad Luck by a short bushwhack; you go almost due west through a natural draw from the point where you first sight Ross Pond on the walk north. It is nearly a mile and more than half an hour to the south shore. The shore of the eastern end of Big Bad Luck Pond is very marshy so it is best to stay a bit south to reach the pond well to the west. Church camp paths lead to the pond, but only to the eastern end, which is very wet, and where campers can launch their boats in order to explore the pond. A camping spot on the north side is difficult to reach without a boat. (Unfortunately, the closest access to Big Bad Luck Pond is directly from an old section of NY 28 via private land, which is posted.)

All three ponds contain fish, but it is difficult to catch them without a boat. Big Bad Luck is known for its bass and pike. Whortleberry is also a shallow pond which has a bass population. Ross Pond is stocked with trout.

Ross and Whortleberry make an easy, short day hike or a pleasant overnight camping experience. The cross-country skiing is rated intermediate because of the hill, but the track is clear and wide enough.

Ross Pond

References and Other Resources

References

Annual Report of the Forest Commission, Albany: Legislature of the State of New York, 1891–1911.
Balk, Robert. *Geology of the Newcomb Triangle*. Albany: University of the State of New York, 1932.
Burroughs, John. *Wake-Robin, The Writings of John Burroughs*, Vol. I. Boston and New York: Houghton, Mifflin & Co., 1905.
Cole, Thomas. *Diary*. Special collection, Library of the State of New York, Albany, NY. Microfilm copy at the Adirondack Museum at Blue Mountain Lake was source for quotations.
Colvin, Verplanck. *Seventh Annual Report of the Topographical Survey of the Adirondack Region of New York*. Albany: Weed, Parsons, printers, 1880.
———. *Report of the Superintendant of the State Land Survey*, Albany, 1897.
Donaldson, Alfred L. *A History of the Adirondacks*, Vols. I and II. Harrison, NY: Harbor Hill Books, 1977. Reprint of 1921 edition published by Century, New York.
Fox, William F. *History of the Lumber Industry in the State of New York*. Harrison, NY: Harbor Hill Books, 1976. Originally published as the 6th Annual Report of the Forest, Fish, and Game Commission, 1901.
Guest book, Warren's Hotel, Schroon Lake Historical Society, Schroon Lake, NY. Microfilm copy at the Adirondack Museum, Blue Mountain Lake, was source for quotations.
Hochschild, Harold K. *Township 34*. Privately printed, 1952. Reprinted in parts by Adirondack Museum, Blue Mountain Lake, NY, 1962.
Lanman, Charles. *Adventures in the Wilds of the United States and British Provinces*. Philadelphia: John A. Moore, 1856.
Longstreth, T. Morris. *The Adirondacks*. New York: Century, 1920.
Miller, William J. *Geology of the Schroon Lake Triangle*, Albany: University of the State of New York, 1919.

162 *References and Other Resources*

Minerva Historical Society. *Minerva, A History of a Town in Essex County, NY.* New York: Multiprint, 1967.
Murray, William H. H. *Adventures in the Wilderness.* Syracuse: Adirondack Museum and Syracuse University Press, 1970. Reprint of 1869 edition published by Fields, Osgood, Cambridge, Mass.
Talbot, William S. *American Visions of Wilderness. The Living Wilderness,* Vol. 33, No. 108. Washington, DC: The Wilderness Society, 1969.
Wessels, William L. *Adirondack Profiles.* Lake George, NY: Adirondack Resorts Press, 1961.

Other Resources

New York State Department of Environmental Conservation (DEC), 50 Wolf Road, Albany, New York 12233
Region 5 Headquarters, Ray Brook, New York 12977
Region 5, Warrensburg Office, Warrensburg, New York 12885
For local rangers, consult local phone books for listing under New York State Department of Environmental Conservation
Adirondack Mountain Club, 174 Glen Street, Glens Falls, New York 12801

For other things to do in the Adirondacks:
New York State Department of Commerce, Albany, New York 12245.
"I Love New York" series: *Camping, Tourism Map, State Travel Guide.*
Adirondack Museum, Blue Mountain Lake, New York

To find your way around the back roads:
Adirondack Region Atlas, City Street Directory, Poughkeepsie, New York, $3.75

Index

Aiden Lair, 47
Adirondack Park Agency, 16
Adirondack Visitors Interpretive Center at Newcomb, 132–133
Bailey Hill, 142
Bailey Pond, 35–36, 42
Bailey Pond Inlet, 42–45
Balancing Rock, 145–146
Barnes Pond, 59–60
Bell Mountain Brook, 157
Big Bad Luck Pond, 156–158
Big Marsh, 38–40, 148
Big Pond, 28–33, 40–42
Big Sherman Pond, 52–54
Blue Ledge, 77, 82
Blue Mountain, 99–100
Blue Mountain Lake, 83, 107
Blue Mountain Wild Forest, 11, 83–102
Blue Ridge Range, 19, 20, 26
Blue Ridge Road, 40, 66, 125, 141
Boreas, 11, 61, 64, 66–71, 137–139, 143–144
Brace Dam, 145
Branch, The, 149, 151
Burnt Mountain, 127
Burroughs Cave, 72–72
Burroughs, John, 55, 72–73
Buttermilk Falls, 103
Bushwhack, 15
Cables, 16
Camping, 16
Casey Mountain, 156
Castle Rock, 106–107
Cedar Point Road, 125
Cedar River, 84–92
Center Pond, 53, 60
Cheney Pond, 135–141
Cheney Pond Overlook, 143

Cobble Hill, 37
Cole, Thomas, 19–21, 26, 31
Colvin, Verplanck, 99–100
D & H Railroad, 66, 70–72, 79, 154–155
Deer Creek, 48
Department of Environmental Conservation, 16
Distance, 13
Durgin Brook, 45
Dutton Mountain, 77
East Branch Trout Brook, 34
East Inlet Brook, 101
Elm Island, 87–90
Essex Chain Lakes, 11
Falls Brook, 52, 54
Forest Preserve, 16
Forked Lake, 119
Forks Mountain, 76–80
Fourteenth Road, 48–50
Goodnow Mountain, 129–131
Grass Pond, 114
Grassy Pond, 74–76
Green Mountain, 52–54
Greyhound Bus Stop, 77, 154–156
Harris Rift Rapids, 80
Hayes Mountain, 42–43
Hewitt Eddy, 61
Hewitt Pond, 55, 59–60
Hewitt Pond Club, 55
High Peaks View Picnic Area, 135
Hoffman Cemetery, 45–46
Hoffman Mountain, 26–28
Hoffman Notch, 38–40, 146–148
Hoffman Notch Wilderness Area, 11, 19, 24, 39, 141
Hoffman Road, 28
Homer, Winslow, 67
Hornet Cobbles, 147

Index

Hot Water Pond, 72–75
Hudson River Gorge, 11, 76–82, 153
Hudson River Gorge Primitive Area, 11, 153
Huntington Forest Nature Trail, 132
Huntley Pond, 82
Hudson River, 76–82, 153–165
Indian Lake, 83, 153
Indian River, 11
Irishtown, 35, 52–54, 141–142
Jones Hill, 32–33
Kettle Mountain, 77, 81–82
Lake Durant, 95, 126
Lake Eaton, 122
Lester Dam, 134
Lester Flow, 137–139
Lindsey Marsh, 60–61
Little Sherman Pond, 52–54
Loch Muller, 31, 34–41, 146
Long Lake, 83, 125–126
Lower Sargent Pond, 103, 108–109, 114–119
Maps, 12
Marion Pond, 35–36, 42–43
Marion River Carry, 108–110
McGinn Mountain, 89–91
Middle Pond, 115–116
Minerva, 47
Minerva Stream, 141–142
Mink Pond, 11, 67
Moose Pond Road, 64, 70–72
Moxham Mountain, 48–51
Mud Pond, 142
Muller Pond, 46
Nate's Pond, 74–76
Natural Stone Bridge and Caves, 19, 20
Newcomb, 125, 132
North Creek, 47
North Point Road, 113–120
North Pond, 28–33
North River, 153
North Woods Club Road, 67–70
Northville-Placid Trail, 126–129

O K Slip Falls, 11, 81
Oliver Pond, 46
O'Neill Flow, 96
Ore Bed Mountain, 54
Owls Head Mountain, 122
Owls Head Mountain Pond, 123–124
Path, 14
Pasley Falls, 84–89
Peaked Hills, 26–28
Pine Mountain, 76–80
Platt Brook, 27–28
Private land, 17
Rankin Pond, 54
Raquette Lake, 109, 115–119
Raquette River, 103, 119
Rich Lake, 132–133
Rock Lake, 92–94
Rock River, 11, 92–95
Rogers Brook, 29, 32
Rogers Pond, 29
Roosevelt Memorial Highway, 47–48
Ross Pond, 156–158
Salmon Lake, 11, 128
Sargent Ponds Wild Forest, 11, 103, 124
Schroon Lake, 19–21
Severance Hill, 24
South Pond, 11, 112
Split Glacial Erratic, 37–38
Stark Hills, 87–94
Stillwater Siding, 72
Stony Pond, 52–53, 59–60
Tahawus, 47, 66
Texas Ridge, 40, 147
Time (of hikes), 13
Tioga Point, 115–119
Tirrell Pond, 83, 95–98, 126–129
Trail, 14
Trout Brook, 19, 21, 34
Unknown Pond, 85–88, 92, 94–95
Upper Sargent Pond, 103, 107–108, 113–114, 118
Vanderwhacker Brook, 11, 66–66
Vanderwhacker Mountain, 64–65

Vanderwhacker Pond, 135
Vanderwhacker Stillwater, 65–66
Vanderwhacker Wild Forest, 11
Vehicular Traffic, 16

Warren's Hotel, 35–36, 42
Washburn Ridge, 39, 43–45
Wolf Creek, 133
Whortleberry Pond, 156–158

SIFP

Books from Backcountry Publications and Countryman Press

Discover the Adirondacks Series
Discover the Adirondack High Peaks, $14.95
Discover the Central Adirondacks, Second Edition $12.95
Discover the Eastern Adirondacks, $10.95
Discover the Northeastern Adirondacks, $9.95
Discover the Northern Adirondacks, $12.95
Discover the Northwestern Adirondacks, $12.95
Discover the South Central Adirondacks, $10.95
Discover the Southeastern Adirondacks, $9.95
Discover the Southern Adirondacks, $10.95
Discover the Southwestern Adirondacks, $9.95
Discover the West Central Adirondacks, $14.95

Other guides to New York
20 Bicycle Tours in the Finger Lakes, Second Edition $9.95
20 Bicycle Tours in the Five Boroughs (New York City), $8.95
20 Bicycle Tours in and around New York City, $7.95
25 Bicycle Tours in the Hudson Valley, $9.95
Canoeing Central New York, $10.95
Fifty Hikes in the Adirondacks, Second Edition $12.95
Fifty Hikes in Central New York, $11.95
Fifty Hikes in the Hudson Valley, $12.95
Fifty Hikes in Western New York, $12.95
Walks & Rambles in Dutchess and Putnam Counties (NY), $10.95
Walks & Rambles in Westchester (NY) and Fairfield (CT) Counties, $9.95

Our outdoor recreation guides are available through bookstores and specialty shops. For a free catalog, write: The Countryman Press, Inc., Dept. APB, PO Box 175, Woodstock, VT 05091.

James C. Dawson and his wife Caroline are active outdoors people who enjoy hiking, cross country skiing, canoeing and fishing in the Adirondacks as well as sailing on Lake Champlain. Jim is best known as an active conservationist who serves as Chairman of the Adirondack Land Trust; as a board member or trustee for The Adirondack Council, Environmental Planning Lobby, Association for the Protection of the Adirondacks and the Lake Champlain Committee; and as a member of NYS-DEC's Forest Preserve Advisory Committee. He is also a past President of the Adirondack Mountain Club. Jim has strong interests in the local history of the Adirondack and Lake Champlain regions, and he serves as Chairman of the Adirondack Research Center of the Schenectady Museum and as President of the Clinton County Historical Association. He is a Professor in the Center for Earth and Environmental Science at the State University of New York at Plattsburgh. His photograph can be found on page 135.

Dennis Conroy retired to North River, New York, from a job with the Agency for International Development in Washington, D.C., where his primary interest was in African economic development. He has travelled extensively in Africa and the Middle East and has lived in Iran, Ethiopia, and Tanzania. He is an avid white-water canoeist and cross-country skier; this, along with a fondness for hiking and camping, brought him to the Adirondacks.

Conroy has written numerous articles on the Adirondacks on subjects such as acid rain, craftsmen, and other people of the region. He regularly reports on Adirondack Park Agency affairs for the magazine *Adirondac*. Conroy has hiked, skied and canoed numerous trips in this book — particularly in the western section. He is currently working with Barbara McMartin as coauthor of a new guide in the "Discover" series on the Northeastern Adirondacks.